A Life Worth Saving

Whoever dwells in the shelter of the Most High will rest in the shadow of the Almighty. I will say of the Lord, "He is my refuge and my fortress, my God, in whom I trust."

—Psalm 91:1–2 (NIV)

Corrine James

ISBN 979-8-88751-269-3 (paperback)
ISBN 979-8-88751-271-6 (hardcover)
ISBN 979-8-88751-270-9 (digital)

Copyright © 2023 by Corrine James

All rights reserved. No part of this publication may be reproduced, distributed, or transmitted in any form or by any means, including photocopying, recording, or other electronic or mechanical methods without the prior written permission of the publisher. For permission requests, solicit the publisher via the address below.

Christian Faith Publishing
832 Park Avenue
Meadville, PA 16335
www.christianfaithpublishing.com

All biblical citations were taken from the New International Version of the Holy Bible unless otherwise indicated.

Printed in the United States of America

Contents

Introduction 1
Romans 15:13—Beauty in a moment 4
Jeremiah 30:17—Will I see her again? 7
Ephesians 1:5—Free to adopt 10
Psalm 27:10—Is this really good? 14
John 8:44—I must have 17
Psalm 100:3—Did God make a mistake? 20
1 Corinthians 14:33—Truth Spoken 24
Jeremiah 29:13—Celebrate Jesus 27
Job 31:15—Mom? 30
1 Kings 19:4—Do whatever it takes 37
John 3:16–17—Abba Father- Yeshua 40
1 Corinthians 6:19–20—How can you hear? 44
Ecclesiastes 4:12—The Lord Speaks 49
2 Corinthians 5:17–19—From my mother's womb He
    has spoken my name... 54
Ephesians 1:6–7—Light still shines in the darkness 60
Romans 8:26—Did you ask me? 63
Matthew 19:14—What's in a name? 66
Exodus 23:20—An angel and an answer to prayer 71
1 Peter 3:15—Proclaim the good news 77
Genesis 2:24—Time to heal 83
Isaiah 43:18–19—The Lord is doing a new thing 90
Matthew 23:26—Women to Women 92
Proverbs 11:24–25—Tenfold 96
1 Kings 19:11–13—That still small voice 99
Proverbs 16:9—Our best laid plans 108
2 Corinthians 3:16–18—The veil has been remove 111

John 17:14–16—The Lord is faithful	116
John 4:6—Vision- Feet on solid ground	119
Psalms 78:6–7—Watch what the Lord will do	123
Joel 2:25–26—Restoration and reconciliation	126
Matthew 6:2—Servanthood?	134
Psalm 4:8—Fear, Anxiety, Depression- How could that be?	140
1 Peter 1:3–4—Eternity in heaven with you	144
Jeremiah 1:19—I am no longer a slave to fear	146
1 John 4:16–18—Lord, how do I love?	151
John 11:35—A year to feel	154
Galatians 2:20—You must first know Me	158
Matthew 7:7—You don't have because you don't ask	163
Proverbs 1:32–33—Why do you call me 'Lord, Lord'?	167
1 Thessalonians 5:16–18—The Lord speaks-A promise given	171
Ephesians 4:15—Truth in Love	175
1 John 4:18—Hands and feet of Jesus- No fear in love	177
2 Corinthians 4:16–18—There is still work to do	180
John 8:36—Free indeed	183
Job 42:10—No longer about me	186
Romans 8:1–2—How can we show God love?	188
1 Corinthians 16:23—The greatest story ever told	191
John 3:16—Free gift	193
Acknowledgments	195
About the Author	198

Introduction

How, then, can they call on the one they have not believed in? And how can they believe in the one of whom they have not heard? And how can they hear without someone preaching to them?

Romans 10:14

Do you ever wonder if your life is worth saving? I mean, do you ever really wonder, *Is my life a life worth saving?* This is something I have struggled with in the past and then again more recently. I have found myself asking this question, "Lord, why would you save me? Why is my life even a life worth saving?"

Out of this question is where this book was birthed. I have had struggles, as we all have. I am even struggling to write this book. It's a miracle I have gotten to this point. I pray the Lord speaks to you through these pages as I partner with Him to give you a story of one that was lost but now has been found, one who is weak but has found strength in Him. I pray you receive it well. I pray, through Him, it speaks to you.

Over the years, I have found that when I am at my weakest point, that is when He is at His strongest. *Second Corinthians 12:9* says, *But he said to me, "My grace is sufficient for you, for my power is made perfect in weakness. Therefore, I will boast all the more gladly about my weaknesses, so that Christ's power may rest on me."* I will boast all the more of my weakness because that is where I will find my strength in Him. Like the old hymn goes, "My hope is built on nothing less than Jesus blood and righteousness; I dare not trust the sweetest Frame, but wholly lean on Jesus name. On Christ the solid rock I stand all other ground is sinking sand."

When the Lord started speaking to me about putting my thoughts down, in preparation for this book, I wondered, *Really, Lord? Me?* I am sure we have all questioned the Lord at one time or another. We wonder, "What do I have to give? Why would you choose me?" We all have a story to tell. Our lives are our stories. I believe that as we share our stories, God will use them to touch others.

Our stories give hope and healing where some may feel there isn't any. In sharing, there is hope, knowing that we are not alone. The question came just as before, "Lord why did you save me?" The Lord quickly showed me, as He always does, that it isn't only about me. It never really is, is it? God always has a plan, and that plan is always bigger.

The Lord loves all of us unconditionally. He loves us all completely and equally. Not one more than another, not one. He loves us all the same. We have a choice to make. We have a choice to choose Him. We have the choice to follow Him and the choice to trust in Him. So why would He save me? Because He loves me, yes, but it's more than that. He also loves my husband, a man who hadn't known Him yet but whom God wanted to reach.

It was about our children and our children's children. It was about the children He knew we would someday have, the children we now have, the children we love yet love so incompletely. His love is complete. It's about the thousands of generations that come after us. *Deuteronomy 7:8* says, *"But it was because the Lord loved you and kept the oath he swore to your ancestors that he brought you out with a mighty hand and redeemed you from the land of slavery, from the power of Pharaoh king of Egypt. Know therefore that the Lord your God is God; he is the faithful God, keeping his covenant of love to a thousand generations of those who love him and keep his commandments."* To the thousand generations of those who love Him. I love Him.

Think about a grandmother, a father, or aunt that prayed for you. A family member that loved Jesus so much that they prayed for you. They wanted you to know and love Him too. What about

Jesus? Jesus is seated at the right hand of God, interceding for you right now. *Romans 8:34* reads, *"Who then is the one who condemns? No one. Christ Jesus who died—more than that, who was raised to life—is at the right hand of God and is also interceding for us."* Even if you didn't have a praying lineage praying for you here on earth, you have Jesus.

God has put it on my heart to share what He has done for me in my life. He also wants you to listen to His small voice and share what He has done in your life as well. *Psalm 145:4* reads, *"One generation commends your works to another; they tell of your mighty acts. They speak of the glorious splendor of your majesty—and I will meditate on your wonderful works."*

The Lord doesn't want us to be like the people we read about *in Judges* 2:10 *"After that whole generation had been gathered to their ancestors, another generation grew up who knew neither the Lord nor what he had done for Israel."* The Lord wants my family, your family, to know all that He has done for us. Just like the Lord *in Judges* wanted all his children to pass down all they had learned and all they had known about Him to the next generation. He wanted them—and He wants us—to never forget.

It's also about you. Yes, you. It's about each and every one of us. He loves us all so much. He loved us all so much that He sent His son. He gave His son's life that we may live. *John 3:16* says, *"For God so loved the world that He gave His one and only Son, that whoever believes in Him shall not perish but have eternal life."* He is showing me how one life, turned to him, can and will affect and impact another one's life. We are not perfect. We are imperfect people who need His grace, His mercy, His love, and His forgiveness. Through our imperfections, we learn and grow; and if we are not afraid to, we can pass all that we have learned to others. As imperfect as our stories may be, they are our stories, His story. Let's read them, live them, share them.

I pray the Lord speaks to you through these pages and brings you peace, healing, grace, and love.

Romans 15:13

May the God of hope fill you with all joy and peace as you trust in him so that you may overflow with hope by the power of the Holy Spirit.

When I was little, I always felt safe, secure, and loved. It was just the three of us. It was my mom, my sister, and me. My earliest memory was when I was as young as four. I remember we had a swing in the backyard that was attached to a clothesline. In our neighborhood, our backyard was connected to all the neighbors on our street. We lived in the lower-income part of town.

I remember that swing. I remember feeling so free. I would swing back and forth, the wind blowing through my hair, my feet hovering just above the ground. I lifted my head back as I moved forward again, my eyes caught the blue sky above. I loved that swing. As I would swing back and forth, I would sing. I would sing so innocently without a care in the world. I would sing about how much I loved my mom and how much she loved me. We didn't have much, but to me, we had everything. What we had was each other.

Fast-forward to many years later, I'm feeling and sensing the same type of peace and contentment in my nine-year-old daughter. I look out the door, getting ready to call her in, but as I look into the yard, something stops me. I see her. She is on the trampoline. I stop for a minute and watch. As I watch her jumping on our trampoline, my mind goes back to me, sitting on that swing so many years ago.

As I watched her, not on a swing but on a trampoline, I see this beautiful peaceful smile shining through. As I watch her little being jumping up and down, I can see the wind blowing through her hair. I see her little feet suspended in the air as they leave the trampoline. She is free. I could see her mouth moving. As I leaned in a little closer, I could hear her little voice singing. I can sense her joy, her peace, her love. She was singing about her family, about her sisters. She had joy. In that moment, she was enjoying just being. The beauty of that day and the peace that flooded over me was an all-encompassing beautiful moment that was just for me that came straight from the heart of the Father.

The peace I saw all around her was simple yet powerful. She continued to sing. I just stood there and listened to her tiny voice. Yes, she too was singing about her family. She was singing about her sisters and the love that she had for them in her heart, and she sang of the love that we had for her. It was simply captivating.

As I stood and watched, I took a deep breath and took in all the sounds and all the smells of spring. It was beautiful of the Lord to show me the same peace that my baby felt right in that moment was the same peace I had felt way back when. The realization of where He had taken me from to where He had brought me to was more than words could ever express. It was beautifully revealed in that very moment in time.

For me, that safety, that peace, and that love would seem to come to an end. I know that for so many of us, it does. Whether it is by a divorce, death, or something else that would negatively impact our lives, whether big or small, something comes and collides with our inner peace, our inner beauty, and our sense of love. Do you know what I mean?

Did you ever have a moment like that? Do you remember what that was for you? It could have been a series of moments or a series of events. There is a time in some of our lives, a moment, that we can look back on and say, "And in that moment, everything changed." I pray my girls would never have a moment like that, but unfortunately, they may.

As people, as parents, we will never be perfect. We will never be good enough. That's why we have Jesus. Jesus is the way to that peace, that love, and that beauty. He is our restorer. If we believe, if we trust in Him, He will restore us. *Jeremiah 30:17* says, *"For I will restore health to you, and your wounds I will heal."*

This world is full of "in that moment" because we are imperfect people living in an imperfect world, but we have hope in a perfect God. *Isaiah 40:31* reads, *"But those who hope in the Lord will renew their strength. They will soar on wings like eagles; they will run and not grow weary; they will walk and not grow faint."*

Jeremiah 30:17

But I will restore you to health and heal your wounds, declares the Lord, because you are called an outcast, Zion for whom no one cares.

The next memory I have is of me sitting in my grandmother's living room. I was maybe five years old. We usually went there every Sunday for Sunday dinner. However, this was not a Sunday, and we were not there for dinner.

My mother had just gotten remarried, and she was standing in the doorway with the man she had married. I really don't remember much of the wedding. I'm not sure I remember it at all. I looked over at the two of them. As I looked up at him, I remember thinking, wondering, *Who is this man?* I didn't fully understand or grasp any of the things that were happening.

As they stood near the door, I knew they were getting ready to leave. I heard them say they were heading off on their honeymoon. I didn't fully understand what that meant. I do remember one thing. I remember the feeling I was having inside my little body. I was feeling nervous, sick to my stomach, confused, and a little uneasy. I couldn't put those feelings into words at the time. I just remember the feeling of sadness, fear, and emptiness. I looked over at my mom; I knew she was leaving.

As I looked up at her, my eyes started to well with tears. I could feel myself begin to cry. The only thoughts that were going through my mind were, *Where is she going? Will she come back?* I wondered, *Will I ever see my mom again?* Even after all these years, as I write, I can still feel that sense of loneliness, confusion, and sadness that I felt on that day. I guess there may still be some healing that needs to take place. Maybe, in writing this book, I will continue to find peace and that healing.

I felt so overwhelmed and afraid. As I began to cry, I could see my mom tense up. I watched her shift her weight from one side to the other. She looked anxious. She glanced at my grandmother, maybe looking for some guidance on how to handle the situation. Now, looking back as an adult, she may have been nervous like me. I'm sure she was probably caught off guard by my tears. She may have been struggling, trying to find the right words—words that would help handle the situation—which would explain her glance toward my grandmother who still hadn't spoken. We had never been apart. Never. It was always the three of us. This was all new for her as well as it was for me. We are all so fragile.

She looked at her mom, my grandmother, again. Then she looked back at me. Tears were pouring down my face by now. I was so afraid I would never see her again. Nervously, she told me to stop crying. I looked at her and tried to stop but just couldn't; it all just made me confused. I tried to look away and looked down at the puzzle in front of me. I felt a tear run down my cheek and hit the floor. My grandmother, not acknowledging me, looked straight at my mom and said to her in a stern voice, "Give a her a good swat on the behind and just leave. She'll be fine." So that's what my mother did. As I watched her walk out the door, something inside me broke.

For the first time in my young life, I learned that it wasn't okay to feel. What I needed in that moment as a child was to be reminded that I was loved and to be reassured that she would be back and everything would be okay. I felt like my mind went blank. I pulled back my tears, stuffed the sadness way down deep, and told myself that it will be okay, that I would be okay. In those few moments, I had convinced myself that I would never see my mother again.

I sat there and began talking to myself, telling myself that I would be fine staying here and living with my grandparents. I looked at my sister. She was older than me, and I thought, *Well, at least I have my sister. I'm not all alone.* I separated myself from my feelings.

My grandmother, then acknowledging me, turned and asked if we wanted something to eat. So we went to the kitchen and sat down, and she made us a sandwich.

When she spanked me and left, I felt empty. My whole sense of security left when she walked out that door. An empty hole that I had never known began to take form inside of me that day. The moment I felt I needed my mom the most, she wasn't there. She had always been there.

My mom did come back and brought with her, her new husband. Our relationship was different though. It seemed to have changed forever. Everything had changed, like so many things in life do. The separation I had felt when she left stayed with me and never left. A separation from what though? Was it a separation from my mother? Was it the separation from my own feelings? Maybe it was a separation from safety. I don't know. But what I do know is that it had all changed in that moment, and I wondered if it would ever be the same.

We moved to a different house, and I started kindergarten. I did feel a glimpse of normalcy when I started school. I went to half-day kindergarten, and when I came home from school, it was just me and my mother. She would always have lunch ready for me when I came home. It was usually a tuna sandwich cut in half, and she would put it on the top step of a stool that she would turn backward. I would sit on the bottom step of that stool in front of the TV, and I would watch *Sesame Street*. That memory of just the two of us brought me peace, hope, and a memory I will cherish.

Ephesians 1:5

In love he predestined us for adoption to sonship through Jesus Christ.

As I grew, things continued to change. We had a new family member. After a few years of my mom being married, we were told that my stepfather had a daughter and she would be moving in with us. She would be my stepsister; however, we were not allowed to call each other stepsisters. My mother would always say, "The only steps in this house are the ones leading up to your bedrooms." She tried so hard to make us feel like a family.

One day, she called us into our room to talk. I thought that was strange because she never did that. We all thought we were in trouble. She sat down on the bed, and she started to talk to us about our family. She eventually got to the point—adoption. She told us that she wanted to adopt our sister (stepsister) and that my father (stepfather) wanted to adopt us. I felt uneasy when she said that, and I thought, *Why would he want to adopt me? He has never even talked to me.* I sat there quietly, wondering, not sure how to feel.

I looked around trying to read everyone else's faces. Everyone was looking down, but my mother seemed convinced that this was going to be great. I didn't think so. I looked at the door expecting my stepfather to come into the room, but he never did. *He wanted to adopt us? Where was he?* He didn't even come in with her to talk to us about this adoption thing. That was like him. Every day, he would come home from work before my mother, and he would walk right by me. He would never say a word. He would just glare at me out of the corner of his eye as he walked by. He never said a single word. He always made me feel so uncomfortable.

I sat there and started to think about my real father. I didn't really know him, and I hadn't seen him in a very long time. But I wondered about him. What was he like? Did I look like him? Was I like him? Did he think about me, wonder about me at all? I think I'd like to know him. I didn't say anything to my mother about what was on my mind, but the next thing I knew, she was talking about my biological father.

She told us that she had spoken to him, and he had agreed to let us be adopted. My mother told us that he had his own family now, and he was happy with this new family. She also told us that he now had a son—the son that he had always wanted. I just sat there. I felt that hole get a little bigger. *A son? The son he always wanted?* I felt sadness and emptiness begin to grow again, getting a little bigger.

I had a father that didn't want me and a stepfather that never looked at me, never talk to me. Yet I had a mother who just wanted us to be a family. I looked at my other siblings as we sat there. I noticed they began to nod their heads in agreement. I felt I had no other choice. So I nodded too. I felt no joy in that room, no peace prevailed.

There was no emotional connection. I felt like that had been broken long ago. It wasn't hard to believe that I really wasn't wanted. It seemed I was the one who was always in trouble, the one blamed for everything. I think they call it a scapegoat in sociology, or maybe back then I was considered the black sheep of the family. Either way, it didn't matter; it was all the same.

One Saturday morning, I was sitting on the floor in the living room watching TV. We had one of those really big swivel TVs that sat on the floor. While I was watching Saturday morning cartoons, my stepsister came in and sat down on the other side. She reached over and swiveled the TV around toward her. I looked at her in confusion. *That's strange*, I thought. *Why would she do that? We could both see.* Confused, I swiveled it back toward me.

She must have gotten mad because the next thing I knew, she had taken a pencil from underneath the coffee table and stabbed me with it. I remember just sitting there watching the blood gush out of my ankle. I was scared. She immediately got up and left the room. I didn't know what to do. I knew if I told anyone, I would get in trouble. Somehow, I knew this was my fault. I looked at it. It was hurting. I could feel it throbbing. I got up and went into the kitchen to get a paper towel. I tried to wipe it off, but it wouldn't stop bleeding. I knew I had to tell my mother.

I quietly headed to their bedroom door, but I stopped. We were never allowed to go in there. I stood there frozen, bleeding. Finally I mustered up enough courage and called out quietly. "Mom?"

She called back, "What's the matter." I couldn't hold back the tears, and I started to cry as I told her what happened. She couldn't really hear me through the closed door, so she told me to come in.

My mom was very upset, and I was immediately taken to the doctor. My stepfather didn't feel like I needed to be seen. He wasn't going to take me. I remember my mother telling him that we needed to and she wanted him to go as well. It was a quiet ride to the doctor's. While at the office, the doctor looked at the wound and asked how it happened. Feeling a little uneasy, I looked at my mother for direction because I didn't know what to say.

I was afraid. I didn't want to say the wrong thing, and I didn't want to get in trouble. She looked at me and told me to tell him what happened. So I did. I tried not to look at my stepfather, but out of the corner of my eye, I could see the look on his face. He was mad. His face was red, and he just glared at me with those eyes that always seemed to look glazed over.

When the doctor treated me, it was painful. He had to get all the lead out so I wouldn't get lead poisoning. The doctor looked at my parents as he worked and asked them why my sister wasn't there to witness what I had to go through. This made my stepfather even more angry. I was treated for lead poisoning, and I was sent home. The ride home was tense. They argued. Although they tried to control the tone of their voices, I could hear what felt like hate coming from the front seat. My mother kept telling him the whole time that they needed to talk to my stepsister and that she needed to be punished.

A LIFE WORTH SAVING

As I looked through the rearview mirror, I could see his face, bright red and angry as always. He looked back at me through that same rearview mirror. I tried to look away quickly, but I caught a glimpse of his eyes. They pierced right through me. He looked at me with disgust, or was it hatred? That's what I felt. When we returned home, no word was spoken to me. I could hear whispering coming from the kitchen, and soon after, I saw my stepfather walk downstairs with my stepsister.

I didn't hear any yelling. She never did get grounded. She didn't even get in trouble. No apology, no recognition, no conversation, no reconciliation—nothing. We didn't speak of it again. I have no idea what was said, but when she walked by me on the way back to her room, she just glanced at me with a little smirk on her face. I still have that scar to this day.

> *But I will restore you to health and heal your wounds, declares the Lord, because you are called an outcast, Zion for whom no one cares. (Jer. 30:17)*

Psalm 27:10

—ṁ—

*Though my father and my mother forsake
me, the Lord will receive me.*

More scars came over the years. When I was a little bit older, one of the punishments that we received is a little hard to talk about. At one point, rice was put on the floor in the corners of the kitchen. We were then told to kneel in the corner on the rice, with our face toward the wall of the room.

I remember trying to move the rice around my knees so I wouldn't have to kneel on it. I would get so dizzy from staring at the back corner of the refrigerator that I would literally feel like I was going to pass out. I would sometimes lean back to sit on my heels, but when I got caught, more time was added to the punishment.

. I remember wanting to talk, wanting to communicate. I remember wanting to have a relationship, but it just never worked out. I felt like my feelings didn't matter. I felt like I didn't have a voice; I wasn't able to speak. I kept everything inside. I felt as though I wasn't able to have any thoughts or emotions.

On my thirteenth birthday, I remember getting called downstairs to celebrate. On the way down the stairs, I could see my parents and my sisters all sitting around the table. In the middle of the table, I could see a birthday cake. I noticed it was a store-bought one which was special to me because we usually made them at home. I half smiled; it always felt awkward when we were all together.

My mother kind of had a tradition. She would sometimes put butter on our noses for our birthdays. I think it had something to do with good luck in the next year. I didn't like it. This year was a little different. I still did have butter on my nose, but for some reason, there was something else added. Not only did I have butter put on my nose, but because I was turning thirteen, they thought it would be fun if my stepfather gave me thirteen spankings. I was shocked. Then I was told to pull down my pants and lie over my stepfather's lap so he could spank me thirteen times. I stood there frozen.

Did I hear correctly? I sort of smiled awkwardly, thinking to myself this must be a joke. They smiled at me and started laughing. "Come on. It will be fun!" In disbelief, I looked around and across the table at my sisters. They were just sitting there, smiling and laughing as I was told again how fun it was going to be. It was explained to me that I would get one spanking for every year I've been alive and the last one would be for good luck. I just stood there.

I started slowly shaking my head no. As I did, I could see everyone start to get annoyed. I looked at them, and it seemed like they were starting to get mad at me. It's like they felt they planned this fun thing to do for my birthday, and they couldn't understand why I wouldn't go along with it. I kept being "encouraged" to pull down my pants. I was told it would bring me good luck. They started to get more annoyed with me. "Come on. I can't believe you're going to spoil the fun!"

I just stood there. I felt like I wanted to cry, but I just held back the tears and told myself it would be fine. I started to pull down my pants, and I laid over my stepfather's lap. I felt humiliated. As I looked over, I caught a glimpse of a smile coming across my stepfather's face. It was awful. I could hear them all laughing and counting each spanking I received. As the last one came, I could hear cheering and yelling, "Harder for good luck!" I felt so embarrassed. Something inside of me broke, it just didn't feel right. How is this supposed to be fun? What am I missing? Why didn't it feel fun to me?

They were all laughing and having a good time, but it felt so wrong. When I got up, I noticed a smile emerge across my stepfather's face again. I guess this made him happy. I quietly sat back down at the table and watched as everyone ate my birthday cake.

There was a piece in front of me, but I didn't want it. I just looked at it. My mother noticed and told me to eat my cake. So I did.

I always felt like I was being told that things were good and right, but inside, those things never felt good or right to me. They felt wrong. I felt like I was always in conflict with what I was being told and how I felt. When everyone was done eating cake, I got up from the table and went up to my room. As I went to my room, I could hear them talking, "What's wrong with her? It's not a big deal. It's all in good fun."

Though my mother and my father forsak me, the Lord will receive me. (Psalm 27:10)

John 8:44

There is no truth in him. When he lies, he speaks out of his own character, for he is a liar and the father of lies.

At some point, my mother realized things were not going as well as she had hoped for and she set up a family counseling session. She tried; she really did. I know she didn't want her marriage to fail. She so much wanted us to be a family. When I heard about the counseling, I felt hopeful. *Maybe, just maybe, I would finally have a voice.* It was quiet as we all got ready to go and got in the car. On the way, my mother tried to engage in small talk. I knew she felt hopeful.

We got to the office, and sat in the waiting room. We sat quietly while we waited for our names to be called for the session. I really had no idea what to expect. I don't think any of us did. I don't remember any of the actual questions, but I do remember at one point, we all started to open up and to be honest with each other. We were all in agreement with something that had to do with my stepfather, but as I glanced over at him, I could see him starting to get angry.

Soon after that, he got up and walked out of the session. We sat there for a little while. I think we hoped he would return, but he didn't. My mother was visibly upset and apologized to the counselor, and she got up and headed for the door. The rest of us followed her straight out to the car. When we got to the car, my mother started questioning my stepfather. She tried to stay calm, but you could see she seemed confused.

She wanted to know why he left. She wanted to know if we would be able to go back and finish the session. There was no response as he backed out of the parking space; the rest of us just sat quietly in the back seat. The silence was deafening. That's how I lived most of my young life—quiet, inward. It seemed whenever I would try to communicate, it just never went well. I sat there reminding myself how I shouldn't have said anything; none of us should have.

Things never really got better. I have one biological sister who is three years older than me. I always wanted us to be friends. I wanted her to be my sister. I longed for relationship. I remember asking her to play with me one day and her telling me no. I was upset, so I told my mother that I wanted to play with her but that she didn't want to play with me. My mother turned around and looked at me and said, "Well, why would she want to play with you? She's three years older than you."

I looked down, walked away, and thought, *Yeah, why would she want to play with me?* We never got close. We never talked. We never hung out together. We never bonded. When I was about twelve, our parents had gone out for the evening and the three of us kids were home alone. My sister and I started arguing about something; I don't even remember what it was. I remember feeling confused about what she was talking about. She was saying that I always cause trouble and its always my fault.

Inside, I felt so uneasy, sad, and confused. I yelled back, trying to defend myself from all the accusations being thrown at me. All of a sudden, I found myself at the bottom of the basement stairs. She had pushed me from the top of the staircase, and I tumbled all the way to the bottom. When I hit the landing, I remember just staying there. I didn't want to get up. I didn't really know what to do. I always lived in fear and confusion. No matter what I did, it was wrong, and no matter what happened, it was my fault. Nothing mattered. I didn't matter.

I looked up at her from the bottom of the stairs, and I yelled, "I'm going to tell mom!"

She said, "Go ahead. You deserved it anyway."

I stopped and thought to myself, *Maybe I did.* I must have done something, but I couldn't think of what it was. I don't know. Was I missing something? I must have done something. Why else would she push me? It's strange; the one that was pushed and sitting at the bottom of the stairs was the one that was afraid of getting in trouble.

When my mother came home, I pulled it together enough to tell her what happened. She was in the kitchen, and I went up to her and quietly told her what had happened. Her response, "Well, I'm sure you must have done something to deserve it. She just wouldn't have pushed you for no reason." I began to believe the lies of the enemy. It was getting so ingrained into my being. I started to think and process all that had happened, and I just couldn't remember anything that I may had done wrong. But there must have been something.

John 8:44 reads, *"There is no truth in him. When he lies, he speaks out of this own character, for he is a liar and the father of lies."* Satan is a liar, and I was starting to believe him.

Psalm 100:3

Know that the Lord is God. It is he who made us, and we are his, we are his people, the sheep of his pasture.

My stepsister and I were only three months apart. We were in the same grade, and we went to school together every day. In high school, we had some of our own friends, but there were some friends that would cross over.

One day, when I was about fifteen, I got on the bus after school and headed home. As I sat down in one of the seats, I looked around and realized my stepsister wasn't there. We never sat together, but she was usually sitting toward the middle of the bus. I thought it was strange that she wasn't on the bus because I didn't remember anyone saying she was going anywhere after school. However, I wasn't always told everything that was going on, so I just assumed she had stayed after or went to a friend's house.

That was not usual, but I assumed someone knew where she was. I got off the bus and walked the rest of the way up the hill by myself toward home. As I walked, I recalled a conversation I had overheard a few weeks before. The conversation was playing over and over again in my head. I had been home alone with my stepfather and my stepsister. I walked down the stairs from my bedroom, and as I rounded the corner to the living room, everything seemed quiet.

As I entered the living room, I could hear voices, like a whisper. Where were they coming from? They seemed to be coming from the basement. As I got closer to the top of the stairs, I thought I recognized my stepfather's voice. *Hm*, I thought, *that's strange. Who would he be talking to downstairs in the basement?* As I got closer, I stopped. It was definitely his voice. I could hear him talking to someone. But who?

I quietly leaned in closer, and the muffled sounds got clearer. I could hear him saying, "You are a real Henry. She is not a real Henry. Do you understand me? They will never be my real children."

I just stood there for a minute. *Is that really what he said? Who was he talking to?* Quickly, I turned back around and walked away. My only thought was, *I knew he never liked me. I knew he never really wanted me.*

Later that night when my mother returned home, I told her what I heard.

It's funny, as much as I knew he didn't like me, I still felt a sadness by hearing it all. All these little things just made the hole inside me a little bigger and a little deeper. It just solidified what I felt about myself. I was nothing. I didn't matter, and I would never be good enough. I could never measure up. My mother must have told him what I heard him saying because later that night, after we were all in bed, I could hear them arguing. They were arguing about me. I could hear my mother say how she could see how he treated me, and it wasn't okay. It wasn't too long after that incident that my sister didn't take the bus home.

When my mother got home from work, she started to prepare dinner like she did every night. When dinner was almost done, she started wondering where my stepfather was. She asked if I had seen him. I said no. She then started to look around. She asked me if I had seen my stepsister. I told her I saw her at school, but she wasn't on the bus ride home. I told her she didn't get off with me.

She wondered why I hadn't told her before. I explained how I assumed she already knew. My mother picked up the phone and started calling around. No one had seen them. She finally got in touch with my step aunt. She was informed that they were both at her house and they were staying for dinner. When she hung up, she seemed relieved to have found them. However, she thought it was odd that they were there for dinner. As the night grew on and they hadn't returned home, she appeared to be concerned again. She called them back to see when they were coming home. When she asked to speak to my stepfather, he wouldn't come to the phone. They didn't come home that night, and that was the last time we saw him.

At school the next day, at my mother's request, I tried to reach out to my stepsister. However, she told me that her father (my stepfather) told her that she wasn't allowed to talk to me anymore. She then walked away with some of her friends trailing behind. I stood there frozen. As I watched her walk away, I realized that I would never be able to hang around with the same friends anymore. If she wasn't allowed to be around me or talk to me, then I couldn't hang around them anymore because she was there. I told myself it was fine; she was closer to them anyway. I distance myself emotionally and physically from them, knowing they would have chosen her over me anyway. I lost a sister that day as well as some friends.

It was tough for my mother. She thought they would eventually come back, but they didn't. The next day, when she came home from work, all their stuff was gone. She cried. I didn't really know what to do to help her. At this point, it was just the two of us; my older sister had gone off to college.

One night, she asked me to sit with her for a while. While I was sitting with her, she shared how she had wondered if things would have been different if I had been a boy. She told me that if I had been a boy, then maybe none of this would have happened. Maybe I could have protected her or stood up for her. She shrugged. Maybe my biological father wouldn't have left; maybe he would have stayed. He had always wanted a boy, a son.

She then told me a story about when she was pregnant with me. She said she had some friends over, and they did a little ritual with a string. They held a string over her belly. If it went side to side or back and forth, whatever the direction of the string, it would reveal whether she was going to have a girl or a boy. The string revealed I was going to be a boy. Her and my father were excited. However, later on in the pregnancy, they found out I was not going to be a boy but rather they were having another daughter.

She shared how my father was disappointed that they would be having another daughter. It was strange as I sat and listened to her telling me all this. You'd think I would be sad, but I wasn't. Why would I be? *Well, of course my father didn't want me. Why would he?* I thought. She continued with the story. While she was pregnant with me, my biological father punched her in the stomach. She wondered if it might have been because they had just found out I was going to be a girl or it could have been because he was drunk. She then wondered aloud, "If you would have been a boy, maybe he wouldn't have cheated on me. Maybe he wouldn't have left me."

I sat there quietly. "Did God make a mistake with me? Was I supposed to be a boy? Was this all my fault?"

> *For God is not a God of confusion but of peace.*
> *(1 Cor. 14:33 ESV)*

1 Corinthians 14:33 ESV

For God is not a God of confusion but of peace.

Does God make mistakes? This is something I began to struggle with. A word was spoken over me. A seed was planted, and Satan had begun to use that word to place doubt and confusion in my life.

My mind and my heart were fragile. *Proverbs 18:21* says, *"The tongue has the power of life and death."* Having this question planted in my mind was not bringing life, it was bringing confusion. *"God is not a God of confusion but of peace."* Remember that.

About this time in my life, I started to reach out to my biological father. I had met his stepson at a dance, and he encouraged me to reach out to him. I picked up the phone one day, and we made plans to meet for dinner. His wife and his son joined us. I remember sitting across the table from my half-brother, and I noticed he was staring at me. I just looked up and smiled at him. He then looked right at me and blurted out, "Why do you have a mustache?" I was shocked. I glanced over at my father then looked down. I was so embarrassed.

I am of Italian descent. That was a physical characteristic that I had, and it was one I was very uncomfortable with. I used to talk to my mother about it, but she just told me that's the way God made me. I didn't know what to do about it or even if there was anything I could do about it. It just added to my wondering if in fact I was supposed to be a boy.

I sat at the table embarrassed, not really knowing what to say. I looked over again at my biological father, hoping for some kind of supportive response. Unfortunately, that's not at all what I received from him. He looked around the table at all of us and said, "Well, it's true. He's not lying." That response made me shrink a little in my seat. It added to my insecurities.

Satan is the author of confusion. What we speak over people matters. What we speak over children matters. Satan takes even those seemingly harmless words, and he twists them. Those kinds of words invoke confusion in young minds. Satan brings confusion where there really doesn't need to be any. These seemingly small things have impact on our minds. They can even follow us into adulthood.

We are all so impressionable. Remember, God does not make mistakes. God does not bring confusion. God created you. He created you in His image, and you are loved. *Genesis 1:27* says, *"So, God created mankind in his own image in the image of God he created them male and female he created them."* Listen, be who you are. Embrace who God created you to be and remember He doesn't make mistakes. He loves you. You are made in the image of Him.

Later, when I became a Christ follower, the Lord put a message in my heart about beauty. This was a message that was for women in the sixteen-to-thirty age group. It was about our beauty within. I was in my twenties, and the Lord was doing a work in my life. I belonged to a church, and I found myself speaking to the pastor's wife about all the Lord was doing in my life. She encouraged me to share the message the Lord had given me with the women of the church. I had never done that before. The Lord confirmed it through prayer. I needed to step out in faith and shared His message. The Lord put that night together beautifully. As I finished the message the Lord had laid on my heart, I looked out at the women sitting at the tables. I began to pray.

In the center of each table, I had placed questions about the topic to encourage discussion. As I looked around, I noticed a lot of the tables and seats were full. Then out of the corner of my eye, I notice one young lady sitting by herself. I prayed and went over and sat with her. As we began to talk and go through the questions, she started to share a little about her college life.

She began sharing about her sisters. She explained how one of her sisters was the pretty one and her other sister was the athletic one. She said she didn't know who she was or how she felt. She really wasn't sure who or what she was or who she should be. I sat and listened. She continued to share how, at college, she was invited to join a group but she began to get confused. She was getting confused about who she was, and she began to get confused about her sexuality. The confusion she was experiencing was not of God; it was from the enemy.

Remember, God is not a God of confusion but of peace. The enemy had found a way. He had planted a seed of confusion. She began to question who she was. I sat and simply shared the truth with her. Our identity is in Christ. It's not in athletics, it's not in our looks, it is in Christ and Christ alone. You are who God created you to be. He did not make a mistake.

Remember, words matter. Let us use them to build each other up, to tell the truth in love. Let's choose our words wisely as we share the truth, encouraging one another in love and lifting each other up. I was there that night to share with her the truth. *John 8:31* says, *"If you hold to my teaching, you are really my disciples. Then you will know the truth and the truth will set you free."* This world has made things more confusing than they need to be. We need to rejoice in who we are in Christ and how God created us. If you have struggled with this, like I have in the past, it's important that you know the truth.

Numbers 23:19 reads, *"God is not man, that he should lie, or a son of man, that he should change his mind. Has he said, and will he not do it? Or has he spoken, and will it not fulfill it?"*

That beautiful young woman to whom I spoke all those years ago is now grown. She is married with two children of her own.

What a blessing it is to see that she grabbed hold of the truth and is passing it down to the next generation.

Jeremiah 29:13

*You will seek me and find me when you
seek me with all your heart.*

I was brought up in the Catholic Church, which is where my curiosity of Christ began. We didn't go to church every week, not even on every holiday, but there were a few things my mother would have us do to bring Christ to the center. One thing we would do was sing happy birthday to Jesus every Christmas morning before we were allowed to open our gifts. That is something I remembered as a child, and it's something I did with my children every once in a while as a reminder of why we celebrate Christmas.

I even followed her tradition of making a birthday cake for Jesus a few times. As I grew, I added new traditions I felt the Lord placed in my heart. I pray my children carry them on. One of the traditions I started at Christmastime was when I purchased an Advent Calendar. It has twenty-five small ornament books that tell the story of the birth of Jesus. It comes inside a larger book that holds all the ornaments.

Every night, starting on the first of December, we sat by the tree; and we would read one of the ornament books that told of the story of Jesus. I also had a pillow advent that had pockets. Every year, I would get small pieces of candy or nuts or chocolate and place one for each of my children in each of the pockets. Each day, after we read from one of the books, we would hang the ornament on the Christmas tree and then one of my children would go and get the candy from the advent pillow and pass them out. We also had a separate box filled with ornaments that had the names of God written on them.

Each ornament explained the different names of God and what they meant. There were twelve, and we would read one of those books every other night leading up to Christmas morning. I loved that time with my children. Every holiday, we made it a point to first focus on Christ. I encourage you to seek out ways to keep Christ in all your celebrations.

At Easter, we would color Easter eggs, but we always bought the package that had all the Christian symbols, keeping Christ in Easter. We also had a dozen plastic eggs. Each egg had a piece of the Easter story that represented the resurrection of Jesus. Every night before Easter morning, we made the Easter story cookies. When done, they represented the empty tomb. As we made them, we read scripture for every ingredient and talk about how it related to what Jesus went through on the cross for us. On Thanksgiving, we focused on thankfulness. We would all share something we were thankful to Jesus for. Simple things but important ways to keep our eyes on Jesus.

When I was in the first grade, I made my first communion. I remember seeing the beautiful pictures of us all in white with our hands in white gloves folded in prayer. I also remember making my confirmation when I was sixteen. I had a neighbor that I babysat for from time to time, and I asked her to be my sponsor. She reluctantly agreed. She wasn't very religious. I remember one time she asked me to go to the mall with her because she had to meet someone. I remember the exchange she made. Looking back now, I realize that it was actually a drug deal. I remember her telling me that her boss wouldn't give her another advance on her salary and she needed the money.

When I was preparing to make my confirmation, what I remember most were the Sunday night classes we had to go to. I loved them especially when we were able to go to one of the youth leader's homes. I remember sitting in her living room, talking about and reading the Bible. I would have liked to do that more often than we did. While we were in the classroom, it was a bit more formal. I remember her talking about Jesus, and reading stories that were all about this Jesus. It ignited something inside of me—curiosity.

I remember thinking to myself, *Who is Jesus?* Every week, she would talk about Jesus and share stories, and every week I would wonder, *Who is this Jesus she keeps talking about?* At the end of class one evening, she asked if any of us had any questions. I got up enough courage, and I raised my hand. "Who is Jesus?" I asked. She looked at me and started to tell me all the things she had said before: He turned water into wine, He healed many people, and she told us things He had said.

For some reason, as I sat listening to her, I felt like there was something more. I felt like there was something I was missing, something she wasn't telling me. So I said, "No, I know all that. I mean who is He? Like who is Jesus really?" She continued to try to explain to me that He was the son of God and that He died for our sins. My mind was trying hard to listen. I was trying to understand, yet there was something I was still missing. As I left, I wondered what that was.

Soon after I made my confirmation, I was in homeroom at school one day, and I looked over at the girl sitting at the desk next to me. I saw "I Love Jesus" scrolled across her book cover. Some girls were looking and snickering at her. She just sat there, looking at her book cover. *Jesus again? What is this all about?* I started asking myself again, *Who is this Jesus and why would she write that she loved him on her books?*

I felt it was a bold statement. He must have meant a lot to her. I mean, I know He is the son of God. I know He died for my sins. I knew it all in my head, but I just didn't *know it yet*. I looked over at the girls snickering at her, and I told them to stop. Who knows? There must be a reason she wrote His name all over her books.

Blessed are those you choose and bring near to live in you courts! (Psa. 65:4)

Job 31:15

Did not he who made me in the womb make them? Did not the same one form us both within our mothers?

When I was fifteen, I moved in with my biological father. As a child of divorce with a stepfather that was no longer in the picture, I think it was natural for me to want to see who I am and where I came from. I know it hurt my mom. She had already gone through a lot in her life, but I needed to see my father and see where I came from.

When I moved in, I began to see so much of myself in him, even the way we looked. I was always taller than my mother and sister, and I had a different face and body structure. I looked more like my father. I even found out silly things that we had in common, like we both liked to drink milk with ice in it.

Unfortunately, not all the things that I found out were good. I noticed we both liked to drive fast. He had a sports car, and if I remember correctly, he liked to drive with his knees. We both had a sense of adventure and a little bit of danger. He had a motorcycle which I loved. I never drove with him, but I knew someday I wanted one. I also noticed he had some anxiety, although at the time I couldn't name it. Yet as I grew into adulthood, I noticed I too struggled with it.

I unfortunately found out the hard way why my parents got a divorce. I know while they were married, he had been an alcoholic although I had never seen him drink. What I did see was his temper. I remember one day, after I had been living with him just a few months, he came after me physically. We were all sitting down at the kitchen table for dinner. On his side of the family, I have a stepsister, a half-brother, and two stepbrothers.

We were all there as well as my stepmother, having pizza together. I had a couple slices, and then I was good. I never was a very big eater. My father looked up and asked me if I wanted another piece. I said, "No, thanks." He looked at me again and kind of laughed then told me to have another piece of pizza. Not even thinking, I responded again, "No, thank you. I'm not hungry." Suddenly, I noticed the room got quiet. I looked up and looked around the table. The room was incredibly still.

I was confused, and I looked over at my stepsister. I asked her quietly, "What's the matter?" But no one looked up from their plates. I looked at my biological father, who was across the table from me, and he looked angry. His voice got loud, and he proceeded to tell me how men like women with a little "meat" on their bones. His voice got even louder as he told me that I was too skinny, and I needed to eat more. Before I knew it, he was up and out of his chair. He was coming at me fast!

Next thing I knew, I was up against the wall in the next room. His face was in my face and my back was pinned against the wall. I looked over his shoulder at the table where everyone was sitting, and no one moved. No one said a word. I glanced down at the floor and quietly said, "Okay, I'll have another piece." I took a step to the side and ducked around him. I quietly walked back to the table, sat down, and ate another piece of pizza.

I stayed living with my father for a while until I found out that I was pregnant. I had been dating a boy a few years older than me, and of course I never thought it would happen to me. But it did. I didn't know what to do, so I talked to a friend of mine, and she suggested we go to a clinic to find out if I was definitely pregnant. We ventured out, but when we got were we thought we were supposed to be, it was closed. We stopped on the way back to my father's house and bought a pregnancy test. I honestly don't know how I felt about being pregnant. I hadn't even had time to process it. I knew I felt alone. I remember telling my boyfriend and a few people at school, and then eventually, I told my father. He didn't say too much.

After I told my father, I started thinking about my time living with him. I had only lived with him a short time, but in that short time, I knew it wasn't a good place to raise a baby. I decided I wanted to move back home with my mother. I felt it was a much safer, quieter place. Staying at my biological father's house with a baby was not the best option. Some time went by, and I finally got up enough courage and called my mother. I never told her I was pregnant. I just asked her if I could move back home.

> *For I am convinced that neither death nor life, neither angels nor demons, neither the present nor the future, nor any powers, neither height nor depth, nor anything else in all creation, will be able to separate us from the love of God that is in Christ Jesus our Lord. (Rom. 8:38–39)*

I moved back to my mother's, but I still hadn't told her I was pregnant. I waited another few weeks. I remember the exact moment I told her. She was in the kitchen; I was near the stairs. I had just gotten to the bottom step, and I stood there. It was kind of a blur. I don't remember the exact words I used, but I do remember her reaction. She was at the sink, and she turned around quick and looked at me. She said, "I can't handle this! I can't take care of another person. You will need to get an abortion."

I just stood there, shocked and in disbelief. I just stood there staring at her. That was not something that had ever crossed my mind. I wondered, *Did I hear her correctly? Did I misunderstand her?* I didn't. She continued to explain to me that I was too young and it would be too much to have to deal with. I stood there; my mind was racing. *Now what do I do? Do I go back to my father's? Didn't she understand that I came home so I could have a safer place to have and raise this baby?*

I quietly looked up and said, "I want to keep the baby." She turned and looked at me. It was like she didn't hear what I just said. "I'm calling tomorrow to get you an appointment." As I turned to walk up the stairs to my room, she called after me, "And your boyfriend will have to come too."

The next day, I went to school. Sitting in homeroom, I looked over at the girl sitting next to me. I knew her. Then, I looked over and saw a friend of mine. She was sitting on the other side of me. I just opened my mouth and blurted out, "I'm pregnant." I don't know why I did. I guess I just wanted someone else to know. Maybe the more people to know, the better? Another one of my friends turned around when they heard me talking and asked what I said. I repeated it. They both looked shocked, and they didn't say too much. I immediately regretted saying anything.

The friend that initially took me to the clinic invited me over her house after school one day. She bought me a gift for the baby. It was a cute little mobile for a crib. It was light tan with cute little bears on it. I brought it home and put it in my room. My mother hadn't mentioned taking me to the clinic in a while; so I thought that she must have heard me, knew my heart, and understood that I wanted to keep the baby. I was convinced that she would help me.

I came home from school a few weeks later, and as I walked in the door, my mother told me she made an appointment for me at Planned Parenthood. She said that she thinks I'm further along than I thought I was, and we needed to get in as soon as possible for an abortion. She told me to call my boyfriend and tell him because she said he needed to come with us. I dialed his number and handed the phone to her. I couldn't talk; I didn't know what to say. I just sort of went blank. I was all alone again. As I walked upstairs, I could hear her talking to him. As I entered my room, I heard the phone hang up.

I began telling myself, convincing myself that everything would be fine. It will be okay. We are going to Planned Parenthood. They council women about this stuff. When I get there, I'd tell them that I want to keep my baby. I knew they would sit down with my mother and me, and they would help us come up with a solution. We would get counseling and some help with the baby. They have options, and they have resources. They will help us. I knew the state helped single mothers. I knew I would be fine, even if my mother couldn't help. I knew my baby and I would be fine.

A week, maybe two went by, and my mother told me the appointment was that day. We got in the car. She drove and picked up my boyfriend. We both sat quietly in the back seat. No one said a word. My mother kept trying to make small talk. I just sat in the back seat, telling myself it would be fine. I wanted this baby, and I knew it would all work out.

When we got to the clinic, I was hopeful. I was hopeful that someone would listen to me. I knew I would be able to tell them how I felt and all would be okay. We sat in the waiting room until I got called to the office. A woman came in and sat across from me. She pulled out a pamphlet and handed it to me. She proceeded to tell me that it wasn't really a baby that I was carrying; it was just a lump of cells.

She told me to sign some paperwork, and she began to tell me what would come next. I quickly stopped her in midsentence, and I told her that I didn't want an abortion and that I wanted to keep the baby. She looked at me puzzled. "Then why are you here? Who brought you?" she asked. I told her my mom did but that I was hoping we could get some counseling. I explained to her that I wanted to keep my baby and asked her if she could help me with other options. She asked me again who brought me to the clinic, and again I told her my mother.

I told her my mom was in the waiting room, and I asked her if she could go get her and tell her I wanted to keep the baby. She looked at me and told me to stay there and she'll see what she can do. I started to feel better. This was going to be fine. I felt at ease. I knew once she talked to my mom, she would come in and we would be pointed in the right direction. I waited and waited. The woman didn't come back.

A little while later, a different woman entered the room. She told me she was taking me to another room. I asked her where my mother was. I told her the other lady was going to get my mom. She didn't know what I was talking about. She told me to follow her, and we went to another room. While there, she took out a johnnie and told me to put it on. I looked at her confused, and I started to panic. I said, "No, wait. Someone is getting my mother."

She looked at me for a minute and told me she would find out what was going on, but I would need to put the johnnie on anyway so they could give me an exam. So I put on the johnnie and sat at the end of the table and waited. About ten min went by and yet another woman came into the room. My heart sank. I began to ask this woman where my mother was. She as well looked confused. She stepped out and came back with another nurse. She told me to lie back in the bed, and she hooked me up to an IV. The room was silent. The nurse looked at me and said, "If your mother brought you here, then there is nothing I can do." She told me to relax, and everything would be fine. As I laid back, I felt tears welling up. All hope left my body.

When I woke up, there were tears running down my face. I looked around and noticed there were other women in the room. They were all lying or sitting up in beds. The beds seemed to line the room. There were so many, all in their johnnies. As I looked around, my eyes stopped as I heard a girl a few beds down asking the nurse how long her recovery would take. She looked to be older than me. Maybe twenties. She told the nurse she needed a timeline because she had a cruise planned with her boyfriend in a couple of weeks and she wanted to make sure she would be good to go.

She asked if recovery would be quicker this time; this was her third abortion. I immediately felt sick to my stomach. Three abortions? I immediately thought, *How did I get here? How did this happen?* The tears dropped to the floor as I leaned over the bed and started dry heaving. In a room full of women, there I sat, empty and alone. Everything was different now. I was different. I lost a piece of myself. It was no longer just a feeling of emptiness; I was numb. Although I know now that she did what she thought was best for me, I felt abandoned. I felt that the one person I should have been able to trust, the person that was supposed to protect me, to listen to me, had not.

The next thing I remember, I was walking out to the waiting room. I saw my mother and boyfriend sitting there. As I got closer, my mother got up, walked over to me, and asked if I was all set. I just looked at her. She then told us she wanted to take us to dinner.

Dinner? She wanted to take us to dinner? I followed her out to the car and got in.

We drove for a while, and she continued to ask us where we wanted to eat. We didn't say a word. She finally pulled into a restaurant and stopped. We walked in and sat down. I stared at the menu, not seeing or recognizing a word on it. The next thing I saw was a plate of food in front of me. I kept thinking, *What is happening here?* I looked over at my boyfriend who was sitting next to me; he didn't even look up. I looked across the table at my mother. She was eating. *How could she be eating?* I thought. *Do neither of them understand what just happened to me? Do they not care?* As I sat looking down, I felt a tear fall from my eye, roll down my cheek, and onto my plate.

> *For you created my inmost being, you knit me together in my mother's womb. I praise you because I am fearfully and wonderfully made. Your works are wonderful. I know that full well my frame was not hidden from you when I was made in the secret place, when I was woven together in the depths of the earth. Your eyes saw my unformed body, all the days ordained for me were written in your book before one of them came to be. (Psalm 139:13–16)*

1 Kings 19:4

While he himself went a day's journey into the wilderness. He came to a broom bush, sat down under it and prayed that he might die. "I have had enough, Lord," he said "Take my life; I am no better than my ancestors."

The next few years of high school were a fog. I had always struggled with feelings of low self-esteem, but after the abortion, my worth was nonexistent. I sank into an even deeper depression. I walked around with it all consuming my thoughts. None of it was ever talked about again.

I never received counseling, I was never asked how I was doing, we never talked about it. It left an empty hole inside of me. I felt unworthy, unlovable. I felt ugly on the inside and outside. I walked to all my classes alone. I would see others walking ahead of me in a group. I would intentionally slow down to keep my distance. I remember one friend would slow down for me; it was the friend who had given me the baby mobile.

She would try to engage in a conversation with me, but I just couldn't. In my head, I always wondered why she would want to walk with me. Why would anyone want to talk or walk with me? She would sometimes ask me to wait for her after class, but I wouldn't. I would either make sure I left before her, or I would linger behind until she left. I figured she just felt bad for me, or she didn't have anyone else to walk with. If anyone did ask about the baby, I told them that I lost it.

I felt shame, guilt, and sadness. This lingered into my adulthood. When I was invited to weddings, functions, and meetings, I would make up excuses to not go. I thought people were just inviting me to be nice. I didn't really believe that they wanted me there. I would decline a simple invite to sit at a table, and I would sit alone. I missed out on a lot of blessings the Lord had for me.

After I graduated from high school, I had no direction for my life. I knew some girls that were going off to college, and they seemed surprised that I wasn't. I was told by the school counselor, as well as my family, that not everyone was meant to go to college; so I took business classes in high school. After high school, I found myself getting up in the morning and getting off the bed, only to move to the couch in the living room.

Every day, I would just lie there on the couch and watch TV. One day, my mother came home from work and told me I needed to get up and get a job. I had no idea where to go. She suggested the department store that was right across the street from us. She told me to apply for a cashier's position. The next day, I got up, got dressed, went across the street, and got a job. Soon after, I was promoted to the office upstairs where I learned receivables as well as the cash office.

A few months later, I became friends with security, and they offered me a job. I switched from my office job and decided to work as security personnel. This is where I met a twenty-six-year-old guy; I was only eighteen. It wasn't a bad relationship. I felt it was the next step to take to get me from where I was to wherever I thought I should be. I didn't want to be at home anymore, so after we had dated for a few months, I convinced him to get an apartment and we moved in together.

It wasn't a loving, healthy relationship. I don't think I even knew what that would look like. I knew the relationship wasn't going anywhere, but I did whatever it took to keep it going. When I was about fifteen, I remembered asking my mother about relationships. Her advice to me was, "Do whatever it takes to make them happy." So that's what I did.

A LIFE WORTH SAVING

There really wasn't any love in it. I just wanted someone to love me. I wanted someone to stay. People told me I could do better, but I didn't believe them. Not that there was anything wrong with him; it was just we weren't the right fit. I couldn't see it. Well, that's not true. I could see it, but I ignored it. What else was I going to do? I would rather be with someone than be alone. I wanted to grow up, and this was how I thought it was done. I wanted to leave and move on with my life.

We did move in together, but the relationship didn't last very long, maybe about a year. He had a friend that he would have lunch with pretty much every day. They were friends, so I never thought about it any other way until one day when my car broke down. I called him for help. He asked me if there was anyone else I could call to help me. He explained to me that he was having lunch with his friend, and if I couldn't find anyone, he would come help but after he was finished his lunch. We broke up after that, and then I was faced with the reality of having to move back home.

I had reached my lowest point. Sometimes, being at your lowest point is the blessing we need to move forward. When we are at our lowest, that is where we can rise. Hitting the lowest point is an opportunity to surrender. Even though we can't see it, it can be the beginning of the most beautiful part of your life. If you let it.

> *And He has said to me, "My grace is sufficient for you, for power is perfected in weakness." Therefore, I will boast all the more gladly about my weaknesses, so that Christ's power may rest on me. That is why, for Christ's sake, I delight in weaknesses, in insults, in hardships, in persecutions, in difficulties. For when I am weak, then I am strong." (2 Cor. 12:9–10)*

John 3:16–17

For God so loved the world that He gave His only begotten Son that whoever believes in Him shall not perish but have everlasting life. For God did not send His Son into the world to condemn the world, but to save the world through him.

I pulled up to the front of my mother's house. As I sat in the car looking over at the front porch, I could feel tears welling within. Soon, they were running down my face. So much regret, so much sadness. *I don't want to be here*, I thought. So much has happened, yet here I sit, right back where I started.

Questions began to pour over me. How can I start all over again? How could I end up right back where I started? I felt like a failure. The thought of walking through that front door was so overwhelming that grief welled up within me and tears began to stream down my face. *What do I have? I have nothing. I am alone.* I sat in the car and began to sob. Emotions crashed over me like tidal waves. Shame, guilt, worthlessness, abandonment, depression—it was all consuming.

I sat there. As tears continued to stream down my face, I began to shout out to God. I shouted out to a God I had once heard of but had not yet known. *Lord, take my life! Just take it! I can't do this anymore! It is all just too much! I'm so, so tired.* The thought of living was too much to bear. I had gone too far, and there was no way back.

Through my tears, I continued to yell at God. I continued to pour out my heart to Him. I had no one else to go to. After a few minutes, I began to hear a soft whisper. The voice seemed to be speaking to me. It said, "Get out of the car." I could hear, but I couldn't fully understand it. *What am I hearing?* I questioned. *Am I losing my mind?* I continued to sob. I heard it again, calm yet steady. "Get out of the car." I settled my emotions a bit as I wondered, *God, is that you?* I immediately started to get angry again. I was so full of anger, sadness, and hopelessness. I remember thinking, *Get out of the car and go where? Where am I supposed to go? What am I supposed to do?*

Quietly, I heard Him again. "Get out of the car."

The steadfast love of the Lord never ceases. His mercies never come to an end; they are new every morning, great is your faithfulness. (Lam. 3:22–23)

I stopped yelling and started to listen. As I continued to sob, I could hear the voice of the Lord say to me, "Call Pamela." Pamela was a girl that I was friends with way back in middle school. When I would go to her house and sleep over, we would have to go to church with her mom the next day. I didn't mind it. I actually really liked it. I remember asking her mom during worship to explain to me what some of the words we were singing meant.

Soon, I began to have a conversation with the Lord. I questioned Him, "Pamela? I can't call her. I haven't talked to her in years! That will be so embarrassing. What would I even say to her? Will she even remember me?"

Again, I heard Him, "Come, get out of the car. Go into the house and call Pamela." With nowhere else to turn, I wiped the tears from my face, leaned over, opened the car door, and walked toward the house.

When I got to the front door, I took a deep breath and opened it. When I got inside the house, my mother was on the couch. That's where she always was. I walked right past her and headed straight for the phone. In a drawer next to the phone was the phone book. I slowly walked into my mother's bedroom, picked up the phone, and dialed my old friend's number.

I was so nervous, so emotional. I had no idea what to expect or what I was even going to say. After a few rings, I heard my friend's voice on the other side of the phone. As I began to tell her who I was and why I was calling, I burst into tears again. Through my tears, I tried to tell her what had happened in the car. I explained to her how I felt someone, maybe even God, tell me to call her.

She immediately told me that I needed to talk to her mom, and before I could respond, she handed the phone to her mother. Her mother listened quietly as I tried to explain. When I was done talking, she invited me to a Christian twelve-step codependency program that she helped facilitate at a nearby church. She invited me to meet her at her house the next Thursday. She offered to take me to the Bible study with her. When the next week came, I got into my car and drove up to her house. I was extremely nervous, but I knew I just had to go.

That night was the first time I heard and understood who Jesus is. I had heard about Jesus in the past, but this time, I fully understood. The Lord opened my eyes and ears to finally hear what the Spirit had been telling me all these years. *Matthew 13:9* reads, *"Whoever has ears let them hear."*

I sat in the meeting and listened to everyone talk about this Father that I had in heaven. I listened and heard about a Father who knew all about me, that knew all that I had been through, yet He still loved me. I learned about a Father that would never leave me nor forsake me, a Father that would never turn His back on me. He had the number of hairs on my head counted. *Luke 12:7* says, *"Indeed, the very hairs of your head are all numbered."*

I had a Father that knew all about my life, knew all that I had gone through, and yet a Father that still loved me. For the first time in my life, I had a Father. I had a Father that wanted me, a Father that gave His life for me, a Father that loved me so much that He sent His one and only son to die on a cross for me. He chose to die for me. He chose to give up His life for this girl that could never do anything right.

He gave His life up for this little girl that no one else could see, a girl that no one else wanted to see. Yet He saw me. I didn't need to be afraid. I was worth more to Him than many sparrows. *Matthew*

10:29 reads, *"Are not two sparrows sold for a penny yet not one of them will fall too the ground outside your Father's care."*

He saw my sin and sent His Son to die on a cross for all of them, each and every one of my sins. He washed me clean, white as snow. *Isaiah 1:18,* reads, *"Come now let us settle the matter," the Lord says, "Though your sins are like scarlet, they shall be white as snow; though they are red as crimson, they shall be like wool."*

I was no longer lost; I had been found.

> *Jesus said to him, "Today salvation came to this house, because this man, too, is a son of Abraham. For the son of Man has come to seek and to save the lost."*
> *(Luke 19:9–10)*

The Lord knew everything about me. He knows everything about you. He loves you still. Receiving forgiveness, extending grace. This is the day I met my Father, my Savior, and my Friend. This is the day a God, One I had only heard of, heard my cry, reached down from heaven, and saved my life. This began a journey of redeeming love, hope, and healing. It would not be easy, but chains would be broken and lives would be saved. *Second Corinthians 5:17–18* reads, *"Therefore, if anyone is in Christ, the new creation has come: The old has gone, the new is here! All this is from God, who reconciled us to himself through Christ and gave us the ministry of reconciliation: that God was reconciling the world to himself in Christ, not counting people's sins against them."*

1 Corinthians 6:19–20

Or do you not know that your body is the temple of the Holy Spirit within you, whom you have from God? You are not your own, for you were bought with a price, so glorify God with your body.

Soon after I was saved, I met my husband to be. At that time, we both worked at a grocery store. He worked full time, and I worked there part time, one day a week. I had seen him and thought he was cute. I remember taking the long way around the store just so I could walk by his department so I could see him. I noticed him talking to this older woman one day, and I decided to ask her about him.

She must have told him of my inquiry because within a few days, he was lingering around the front of the store where I worked. I could see and hear him talking to the managers about a new car he had just purchased, a gray Mustang convertible. He turned back around and walked toward the registers again and came through my line. He looked at me but didn't say a word; he just smiled.

I could tell he wanted to say something, but he was too nervous. When I was getting ready to leave, I noticed him looking over at me, and as I started to walk toward the door, he began to walk toward me. We got out to the parking lot, but he still said nothing. Not wanting him to leave without saying a word, I quickly tried to think of something to say. I didn't have much time, and I blurted out the only thing that came to my mind. "Hub caps or wheels?"

I had overheard him talking about that earlier in the night; however, I had no idea what it meant. It makes me laugh when I think of it! He stopped, turned around, smiled, and waited for me. As we walked through the parking lot together, I listened to him talk all about his new car. It was a nice car. However, I didn't really care about his car and I had no idea what he was even talking about. That night, we sat in his new car in the parking lot for hours, just talking and laughing.

It was getting late, and I needed to get home so I made sure I gave him my number before I left. He called a couple days later and asked to see me on the upcoming Saturday. I was so excited, I said yes right away. But after we hung up the phone, I realized I didn't want to wait that long to see him, so I called him back. I asked if he was available to get together sooner. Bold, I know. He kind of laughed and said sure.

For our first date, we met halfway between our houses, and from there, we took his car. The date consisted of him taking me to the farm he worked at to see the goats and animals and then he took me out for ice cream. Easy and simple. We both ordered black raspberry ice cream, which happened to be our favorite. It was a perfect first date.

I talked about Jesus a lot. I found myself wondering at one point what he thought about me always talking about Jesus. *Does he think I'm nuts?* I thought. *I don't think so because he is still dating me!* He never stopped me from talking about Jesus. He never said a negative word about it. He would just listen. Jesus filled my heart. He was all that was in me, and He just poured out of me naturally.

I would share what I was reading, what I was learning, and what God was showing me, teaching me. He just kept coming around! I finally came out and asked him, "Is it strange to you that all I talk about is Jesus? Why do you stay with me when Jesus is all I talk about?"

His response was honest and simple, "I don't really know. There's just something about you." I chuckled to myself a little as I thought about the Holy Spirit, knowing that it had nothing to do with me but had everything to do with what the Holy Spirit was doing.

My new boyfriend wasn't saved. He was raised in the Greek Orthodox Church, but he never really went. He and his family would go on holidays and special occasions. It was an important tradition for them, but he never really made a commitment to follow Christ. Soon after we began dating, I invited him to church. He agreed to go with me and began coming to church with me every week.

Some of the people at the church who were my mentors were a little concerned for me. They knew how much I had been through and how much the Lord had brought me through, and they didn't want to see me slip away from the church, from God. They had seen it happen too many times. A follower of Christ would start a relationship with someone who didn't know the Lord on a personal level, and they would slowly be pulled away in a different direction. Usually, the Christ follower would eventually stop coming to church.

What I loved about my church family is even though they may have had concerns, they loved and embraced him anyway. They reached out to him and loved him. He always felt welcomed. God knew, and I knew in my heart that he would be saved and that he was the one for me. I needed someone who would love the Lord. Everyone's walk with Jesus may look different, the way we love God, the way we relate to God; but God wanted me to have someone who would worship and serve with me. He wants that for all of us. God's design is that we are able to share our whole life not just a piece of it. God is a big part of my life.

He first started coming to the twelve-step program I was a part of. We went every Thursday night together. We soon joined other Bible studies. It was a blessing to share my faith and to grow in faith with someone God had chosen for me. He would have to drive past the church every Sunday morning to pick me up, and then we would drive back to the church together. He was like that. Whether it was for church or for a Bible study, he would just automatically pick me up. He started to get involved more and more on his own in the church. Even more than I was. He drove the van every Sunday, he joined the worship team, and later, we were youth leaders together.

A LIFE WORTH SAVING

We chose to be around older Christians, joining Bible studies and prayer groups. We wanted to grow. They were always so welcoming. They never judged and always loved. We pulled up to a house for the new Bible study we joined. It was cold outside, so we sat in the car and finished the last bit of our cigarettes. Nervously, we went inside and handed them our coats. No one mentioned anything about us smoking, but I knew they must have known.

A few years later, after we were married, we joined a marriage group. Weeks into the study, we were asked to lead the next section. I was surprised because we were a young couple, but we were told we would bring a different perspective. I was superexcited and couldn't wait to dive into the material and see where God wanted us to go with it.

As we sat praying and preparing, disappointment started to creep in. Nothing was coming to our minds. God was not speaking. Frustrated, we turned our focus away from seeking the Lord about the study to asking the Lord why we weren't able to hear from him. Immediately the Lord spoke, "How can you hear me through all of this smoke?" The Lord brought conviction.

Tears began to well up and roll down my face as the Lord continued to speak, "Your body is the temple of the Holy Spirit." *First Corinthians 6:19–20 says, "Or do you not know that your body is the temple of the Holy Spirit within you, whom you have from God? You are not your own, for you were bought with a price. So, glorify God in your body."* The truth resonated deep within; we both began to repent.

My husband got up, took our cigarettes, and threw them in the trash. As I saw them lying there, a huge sense of loss flooded over me. Those cigarettes were my best friend. They had gotten me through so much. What was I going to do without my friend? Jesus spoke, "I am your friend." *John 15:14–16 says, "You are my friends if you do what I command. I no longer call you servant because a servant does not know his master's business. Instead, I have called you friend, for everything that I learned from my Father I have made known to you, you did not choose me, but I chose you and appointed you so that you might go and bear fruit—fruit that will last—so that whatever you ask in my name the Father will give you."*

Later, after we had quit smoking, I asked the facilitator of the Bible study why they never said anything about our smoking, "Clearly you knew?" Her response was "It's not my job to change you. I've learned to leave that up to Jesus."

Ecclesiastes 4:12

*Though one may be overpowered two can defend themselves,
a cord of three strands is not quickly broken.*

After our first date, we saw each other every single day. We would go get a coffee or go to a Bible study; it didn't matter. We would just hang out. About six months into our relationship, he started a conversation about marriage. At that point, I had to be honest with him. I told him that it was very important that I commit my life to someone who loved Jesus. I couldn't marry someone who hadn't given his life to Christ. *Second Corinthians 6:14* says, *"Do not be unevenly yoked to unbelievers."* This scripture spoke to me. It is important to be with someone you can speak the things of God with, someone who has understanding and oneness in Christ.

If I was going to marry someone, it needed to be someone I was going to be spiritually yoked to. That is God's design. I wanted to grow together in the Lord. Even fail together. The Lord needs to be at the center of any marriage no matter how perfect or imperfect we may be. With God at the center, with God in both of our lives, I knew we would make it. If I was going to enter a covenant relationship as important as marriage, it needed to be with someone who knew the Lord, someone who would pray with me and for me, someone to share my/our faith.

When I told him how I was feeling, he immediately told me that he had already made a commitment to follow Christ. I was a little shocked. "When? Why didn't you tell me?"

His response was simple: "Because it was between me and God." He had said a prayer of repentance and received forgiveness one Sunday when the pastor asked the congregation to bow their heads and pray. He gave everyone the opportunity to receive Jesus as their Lord and Savior if they wanted to. He had quietly made that commitment and followed the pastor as he led the congregation in a prayer. He had given his life to Christ.

Soon after, he asked me to marry him in the parking lot of Dunkin' Donuts. I know that doesn't sound very romantic; but it's where we spent most of our time sitting in his car, drinking coffee, and talking. We started planning our wedding and saving money, and we started premarriage counseling. We were excited to start our lives together. As the plans progressed and we started to discuss the wedding, my in-laws-to-be seemed to be less and less happy with our choices.

I shared earlier that my husband is from a Greek Orthodox family that is drenched in tradition. When they heard we were getting married in the Protestant Church, they were not happy, which was a surprise to us. We went to church every week together and we were growing in our faith. His parents wanted us to experience the same traditions they did at their wedding, and they wanted us to be married in the Greek Orthodox Church.

His mother had been Catholic. When she met my father-in-law, she converted to the Orthodox faith and then married her husband. They expected the same from us. This had never been a thought in our minds, never a question for us, where we were going to get married. The church we were going to was the church we learned about Jesus and gave our lives to Him. It was the church we made the commitment to follow Jesus. It was our church. It was the church we wanted to make our marriage commitment to each other in.

It was never a discussion. Why would it be? We both knew. However, it created a rift between his family. I remember going down to his basement to do our premarriage counseling, on our way down the stairs, his father became angry. He told us we weren't allowed to read that Bible in his house. Later, his father told him he disowned him. The rift between his family because of where we were getting married had gotten so bad that his mother took pictures off the wall of all the family members that supported us.

We were at his house one day, and the discussion of our marriage came up. I was told by his parents that I wasn't good enough to marry their son. I was crushed. This is the family that I had spent the last year and a half with. We hung out together, played cards, went for Friday night dinners. It was awful. If anyone reading this can relate, I am so sorry that you had to go through that. It is hurtful. We were all hurt. I was hurt because I had taken them in as my family, and I felt like they had to. But I was wrong. I felt they had turned their back on me, like everyone else eventually did.

They said horrible things. Not only did they tell me I wasn't good enough to marry their son but they also told me I wouldn't make a good wife or a mother because I came from a broken home. I was told that my mother must not love me very much if she expected me and their son to pay for our own wedding. I was told if she loved me, she would have planned better. To them, I was raised by a single mother. Therefore, I would not make a good wife or mother. It was a low blow. I left that day, and I decided I wasn't going back.

Matt and I were still together, but I had not gone back to his parents' house for a few months. When I worked in the area, I would go to his house and pick him up but never went in. On one of those occasions, as I pulled into his parents' driveway, he came out of the house and asked me to please come in. I looked at him in shock. He again asked me if I would go in and talk to his parents. I couldn't believe what he was asking me to do. I refused.

He explained to me how things had really gotten bad in his family, and I needed to come in and help make it better. I couldn't believe what I was hearing. *I needed to make it better?* I was so hurt and angry. How dare he ask me to go inside and help make things better! Why would I do that? I didn't do anything wrong! I sat in the car and refused. He just kept looking at me with a look of desperation I had never seen before. "Please come in with me," he said. I could tell he was hurt and lost. I sat in the car, nervous and upset. I asked him to give me some time alone to pray.

I sat in the car and watched him go back into the house. As I sat there, I began to cry. I was so hurt. I started to pray and cry out to the Lord. Through my tears, I began to hear Him speak. "Go apologize," I heard Him say. I was a bit taken aback by what I heard Him say. *Wait, what?* I thought. *Was God talking to me?* Again, I heard Him say, "Go apologize."

Tears began to well up again. I didn't understand. "Lord, why would you ask me to do that? Why would you ask me to apologize?" All the feelings of insecurity and low self-esteem flooded over me. "Lord, why would you tell me to apologize? You know I didn't do anything wrong. Don't you know what they said to me? All the horrible things they said to me. Don't you care?" I wondered, *How could God asked me to reach out to someone who had been so awful to me. Lord, why me?*

Quietly, He spoke again, "I need you to be my hands and my feet. I need you to do what they cannot. I need you to go, in my name, and break the chains of unforgiveness in the spiritual realm. They are not able to." I sat quietly. The Holy Spirit was speaking to me, and I began to listen.

"Okay, Lord, I will go and apologize. But what am I going to say? What am I going to apologize for?" I asked.

He answered simply, "For the situation."

Immediately, my eyes were opened, and I saw everything clearly. I understood the situation. It had nothing to do with me. It had to do with a family that needed help, and they didn't know how to bridge that gap. "Yes, Lord," I answered. "I will obey." I wiped my tears, got out of the car, and went inside.

Matthew 5:23–24 says, *"Therefore, if you are offering your gift at the altar and there remember that your brother or sister has something against you, leave your gift there in front of the altar. First go and be reconciled to them, then come and offer your gift."* This scripture has always stood out to me because it says if we know that someone holds something against us, then we go and be reconciled.

I found his dad sitting at the table like he always was. I said hi to him as I walked by. I headed right into the living room where I knew I would find his mom. There, she was sitting on the couch. I went to her, bent down on my knee, face to face, and apologized for all that had happened and for all that was going on in her family. I leaned in for a hug, which she returned. She immediately stood up and said, "Let's go play some cards." We walked into the other room and sat down at the kitchen table. She dealt those cards out like she had done so many times before. It was like nothing had happened.

Some years had gone by, and we had our first child. We were invited to my in-laws for dinner, so we went. I remember my father-in-law looking up at me from across the table. He looked at me and simply said, "Sometimes, people say things they shouldn't say, and sometimes, people say things that they don't mean." He looked up at me, "Do you know what I'm saying?" I looked at him, and our eyes met. I didn't really know where he was going, but I knew it was time to listen. He looked down and then back up again at me and continued, "You're a good mother." In that moment, the years came flooding back to me. I looked at him and realized what he was saying. This was his apology for all those years ago. This was what he could give. In that moment, I understood, and it was enough. The peace of the Lord filled that moment. I looked up at him and smiled. We both knew.

2 Corinthians 5:17–19 ESV

Therefore, if anyone is in Christ, he is a new creation. The old has passed away; behold the new has come. All this is from God, who through Christ reconciled us to himself and gave us the ministry of reconciliation; that is, in Christ God was reconciling the world to himself, not counting their trespasses against them, and entrusting to us the message of reconciliation.

When I was saved, there was one thing that God had dealt with right away. It was that He knew everything about me, and He still loved me. He loved me right where I was. The Bible says He knows everything about us. He even knows the number of hairs on our heads. *Luke 12:7* says, *"Indeed, the very hairs of your heads are all numbered. Do not be afraid: you are worth more than many sparrows."* He knew all my thoughts and all my struggles, and He loved me anyway. He loved me unconditionally.

After I had been saved for a while, I joined a Bible study with a group of women. We gathered together to share our lives. That was so important to me. I needed to find some Christian friends to do life with, friends that would lift each other up, love each other, and encourage each other in the Lord, to be there for each other. *Proverbs 27:9* reads, *"Perfume and incense bring joy to the heart, and the pleasantness of a friend springs from their heartfelt advice."*

Those relationships are where truth, healing, and love come from. This is where the truth about my first child began to come to light for the first time since I had made a commitment to follow Christ. This is where I found another who had walked a similar jour-

A LIFE WORTH SAVING

ney, one who was also in need of healing. We heard about a group of women who were holding a Bible study that was about an hour away. It was a study for women who had previously had an abortion. It was a study that would bring healing, truth, and forgiveness. We walked through this journey together.

Each week, the two of us made the commitment to pick each other up and drive to the study together. Some rides were quiet; some were tearful. *Romans 12:9—10* reads, *"Love must be sincere. Hate what is evil: cling to what is good. Be devoted to one another in love. Honor one another above yourselves."* Don't we all need someone to walk beside us in this life? This was the safe place where I was finally able to grieve the loss of my unborn child. The Lord was there. He had not left me. He spoke to me and comforted me.

Every week, we worked through our loss as we walked through our journey together. We all had different stories. When we progressed to the end of the study, we were encouraged to name our babies, the babies that we didn't get to meet here on earth. I prayed to the Lord for my child, for His child. As I prayed, I sensed that I had conceived a baby girl.

While I continued to pray, I asked the Lord what name He had for her. After a few days of seeking the Lord, one name kept coming to the forefront of my mind—Christina. Christina was the name the Lord had given her. I later looked up the meaning of Christina. It means follower of Christ.

Isaiah 49:1 reads, *"Listen to me, you islands; hear this, you distant nations: Before I was born the Lord called me; from my mother's womb he has spoken my name."*

I finally was able to place my daughter in the arms of Jesus. She had been there all along. She is with the Father, her Father. She is safe. She is loved. She is resting in the arms of Jesus. She is sitting at His feet, and I will see her again. *John 1:5* says, *"The light still shines in the darkness and the darkness has never put it out."* She is living in the light of Jesus; and I take comfort in knowing, someday, I will see my baby's face and we will spend eternity together forever.

John 14:1–3 (ESV) says, *"Let not your hearts be troubled. Believe in God, believe also in me. In my Father's house are many rooms. If it were not so, would I have told you that I go to prepare a place for you? And if I go and prepare a place for you, I will come again and will take you to myself, that where I am you may be also."*

I still have that study book, and I still have the rose from the rose ceremony we had for the babies. Our babies. I will treasure it. When the study ended, each of us was given these beautiful messages:

You may not know me, but I know everything about you. (Psalm 139:1)

I know when you sit down and when you rise up. (Psalm 139:2)

I am familiar with all your ways. (Psalm 139:3)

Even the very hairs on your head are numbered. (Matt. 10:29–31)

For you were made in my image. (Gen. 1:27)

In me you live and move and have your being. (Acts 17:28)

For you are my offspring. (Acts 17:28)

I knew you even before you were conceived. (Jer. 1:4–5)

I chose you when I planned creation. (Eph. 1:11–12)

You were not a mistake, for all your days are written in my book. (Psalm 139:15–16)

I determined the exact time of your birth and where you would live. (Acts 17:26)

You are fearfully and wonderfully made. (Psalm 139:14)

I knit you together in your mother's womb. (Psalm 139:13)

And brought you forth on the day you were born. (Psalm 71:6)

I have been misrepresented by those who don't know me. (John 8:41–44)

I am not distant and angry but am the complete expression of love. (1 John 4:16)

And it is my desire to lavish my love on you. (1 John 3:1)

Simply because you are my child, and I am your Father. (1 John 3:1)

I offer you more than your earthly father ever could. (Matt. 7:11)

For I am the perfect father. (Matt. 5:48)

Every good gift that you receive comes from my hand. (James 1:17)

For I am your provider and I meet all your needs. (Matt. 6:31–33)

My plan for your future has always been filled with hope. (Jer. 29:11)

Because I love you with an everlasting love. (Jer. 31:3)

CORRINE JAMES

My thoughts toward you are countless as the sand on the seashore. (Psalm 139:17–18)

And I rejoice over you with singing. (Zeph. 3:17)

I will never stop doing good to you. (Jer. 32:40)

For you are my treasured Possession. (Exod. 19:5)

The Lord is faithful, He is loving, and He is just. I still think of my daughter. I think of her often. I think of her when I see my three girls, and I know they have an older sister that they will never meet this side of heaven. I think of her when we sit at our dinner table that seats six. There is always an empty seat. One person is missing at the table.

Many years later, I was at a Bible study in a completely different church with completely different people. I was invited to join, and everyone else in that study were family. All except me. One of the women was pregnant. She shared for the first time with her family, through tears, that she had an abortion many years ago. She shared how she was anxious about the health of the baby. She was thinking she didn't deserve to have this child. She worried that something would happen to him before she could give birth because of what she had done earlier in her life.

As I listened, it became clear that she had all the same concerns I had when I was pregnant with my second child. All the fear that fills us because of the truth of what we know we deserve opposed to the grace, forgiveness, and love that the Lord chooses to bestow on us. As I sat there in this new group of women, I felt the Lord nudge me. I shared with her my story. I shared how her child, the first child that she conceived, was safe in the Father's arms and we would someday see our babies again. A weight was lifted. The Lord is good, and His mercies are new every morning.

Psalm 103:8–12 says, *"The Lord is compassionate and gracious, slow to anger, abounding in love. He will not always accuse, nor will he harbor his anger forever; he does not treat us as our sins deserve or repay us according to our iniquities. For as high as the heavens are above the earth, so great is his love for those who fear him; as far as the east is from the west, so far has he removed our transgression from us."*

Ephesians 1:6–7

To the praise of his glorious grace, which he has freely given us in the One he loves. In him we have redemption through his blood, the forgiveness of sins, in accordance with the riches of God's grace.

Years later, I would become pregnant again, the first pregnancy that I was able to carry to full term. It seemed to take a while before we were actually able to conceive. At first, doubts and fears began to rise up within me. I wondered, *Will I be able to become pregnant?* Thoughts of what had happened years ago would flood back to my mind and to my heart. Those thoughts would try to undo what the Lord had already done for me—forgive.

My husband and I served as youth leaders at our church. Most of the youth leaders we served with were around the same age as us. One by one, each couple announced that they were expecting. We, even though we were trying, still had not. Those doubts and fears came rushing to the forefront of my mind. I began thinking, *I don't deserve to have a child. I don't deserve to be a mom.* I started to settle into the thinking that if I wasn't able to conceive, I would understand. I didn't deserve to have a child. I began to forget the God of grace.

We receive forgiveness and yet we are so quick to forget it and we start carrying the burden all over again. *Matthew 11:28–30* reads, "*Come to me, all you who are weary and burdened and I will give you rest. Take my yoke upon you and learn from me, for I am gentle and humble of heart, and you will find rest for your souls. For my yoke is easy and my burden is light.*"

A LIFE WORTH SAVING

We sometimes forget too quickly that God is a God of mercy and grace. We forget what is written in *1 John 1:9*—*"If we confess our sins, he is faithful and just and will forgive us our sins and purify us from all unrighteousness."* The Lord does not change. His forgiveness is His forgiveness. *Micah 7:19* reads, *"You will again have compassion on us; you will tread our sins underfoot and hurl our iniquities into the depths of the sea."* Thank you, Lord! Let us not pull them out again! *Hebrews 8:12 (ESV)* says, *"For I will be merciful toward their iniquities, and I will remember their sins no more."* This is who our God is. Let us not forget.

I did become pregnant, just about three months behind the rest of the youth group leaders. I remember that first ultrasound we went to. I was focused and waiting in anticipation of the sex of the baby. I had always prayed for daughters. I did not grow up with boys—no brothers, no fathers, no cousins, no boys. I wouldn't have the first clue what to do with a boy. I didn't know the first thing about having or raising boys! I was definitely praying and hoping for a girl.

While I was lying on the ultrasound table, the tech put the gel on my stomach and I turned my head to see the first image of our child. As she moved the device around my stomach, she began to point out every inch of the baby: the head, the legs, the fingers, the toes. As I watched, I began to get less and less excited about the sex and began to look more intently at the features that were so prevalent on the ultrasound. Everything looked so perfect. I could see the head and the feet, but not only that, I could see the eyes and a nose and the shape of this baby.

I began to get a bit of an unsettling feeling. As I looked, I realized, this is a baby. This baby is growing inside of me. We left the appointment with an ultrasound in hand. It revealed that we were having a baby girl. I felt humbled. The Lord answered my prayer. We were both excited to bring this beautiful little girl into the world.

As we drove home from the appointment, I continued to look at the ultrasound. I felt this strange uneasiness all over again. As I looked at that growing, forming baby in my belly, I remembered the words of the women from Planned Parenthood: "It's not a baby anyway. It's just a clump of cells." Those words replayed in my heart, in my mind, and in my soul. I looked down at that picture of my baby, our baby, and I began to sob. The realization of the lie that was told to me so many years ago was overwhelming.

The next morning, as I sat spending time in my devotional, I picked up that ultrasound picture of my baby again and began to weep. I wept again for the child that I had lost. I began weeping for the many women like me who went to Planned Parenthood for help and were taken in a direction that maybe they, like me, never intended nor could have imagined. I thought about how many other women had been lied to by the very people they wanted help from. How many women were told that their precious baby that was growing inside them was not actually a baby but just a lump of cells?

Women, so many women, have been lied to for far too many years. Many women, if they were given the truth, if they were given the chance to see their precious babies, would have never made the decision that they made on that day, the decision to terminate their pregnancy. My husband shared a memory he had from high school about a couple who had become pregnant and later decided to terminate. He shared with me how his friend was never the same.

I wept that morning for all those women, for all those men who lost their children. I wept for all those women who believed the lies that were told to them. I wept for the women who would later have the truth revealed to them, whether in the revelation of their own baby's beautiful ultrasound picture or that of a loved one. I wept for the children; I wept for humanity. I felt a nudge to find out the meaning of my name, Corrine. I took a drive to the Bible store and found a card with my own name on it. My name means maiden. Underneath the name was a scripture that read, *"The light still shines in the darkness and the darkness has never put out the light."*

First Timothy 1:15–16 says, *"Here is a trustworthy saying that deserves full acceptance: Christ Jesus came into the world to save sinners-of whom I am the worst. But for that very reason I was shown mercy so that in me, the worst of sinners, Christ Jesus might display his immense patience as an example for those who would believe in him and receive eternal life."*

Romans 8:26

*In the same way, the Spirit helps us in our weakness.
We do not know what we ought to pray for but the Spirit
himself intercedes for us through wordless groans.*

Our firstborn graced our presence on September 16, 1998. She was perfect. With her birth came joy, healing, and forgiveness. While I was still pregnant, I applied what I learned from the experience of my first pregnancy and the healing process that followed.

What I learned was how important names are to God. Our names are incredibly important to our identity. God named the first man Adam, which means son of the earth. *Genesis 2:7* reads, *"Then the Lord God formed a man from the dust of the ground and breathed into his nostrils the breath of life; and the man became a living being."* Then in *Proverbs 22:1 (ESV)*, it is said, *"A good name is to be chosen rather than great riches, and favor is better than silver and gold."*

God changed Abram to Abraham, Sarai to Sarah, Jacob to Israel, and Simon to Peter. While I was carrying our firstborn, I prayed for my unborn child. I prayed for her by name. I had decided a long time ago that if I was to ever have a daughter, I would call her Michaela. When I was younger, I babysat for my neighbor, and she had a little girl named Mikayla. I always loved that name; and I told myself that one day, if I have a daughter, that is what I will name her.

As I spent time with the Lord one morning, I felt led to pray for Michaela specifically by name. While I was praying for her, I heard the Lord speak. "Did you ask me?"

I thought, *What a strange question, Lord.* I put the thought aside and continued to pray.

I heard Him again. "Did you ask me?"

Again, I put the question aside and continued to pray. God continued with persistence. After a few more times of hearing the same question, I realized that yes, indeed, this was the Lord. I began to acknowledge Him and recognize His voice fully. I responded, "Ask you what, Lord?"

He quietly answered, "What I want to name her?"

I immediately felt the presence of the Holy Spirit. I remembered how important names were to God, yet over time and during this pregnancy, I was so fixated on what I wanted to name her that I had forgotten to seek the Lord on this one. I humbly asked for forgiveness and then proceeded to ask the Lord what name He had for her. He gently responded, "Have you looked up the name Michaela?" I put down my pen and looked up the meaning of her name. Michaela—"who is like the Lord."

I immediately felt peace within my soul and rejoiced like never before! The Lord is so good to me! *Psalm 136:1 (NKJV)* reads, *"Oh give thanks to the Lord; for He is good; His mercy endures forever."* He knew my heart. He loved me. He was just wanting to confirm in me what He had already placed in my heart. Later that day, I spoke with my husband and told him all about my conversation with the Lord. His response, "It's settled. Michaela is her name." As she grew, she grew to love the Lord.

Michaela prayed and gave her heart to Jesus when she was only three-and-a-half years old. I remember we were driving in the car, and I had worship music on. We were singing about Jesus and talking about how much He loves us. She has the most beautiful eyes that would sparkle whenever she smiled. My brown-eyed girl. As we drove, Michaela said to me, "Mommy, I want to know Jesus! I want to have Jesus in my heart!" I looked in my rearview mirror and saw those beautiful brown eyes sparkling. I asked her if she wanted to pray, and she said yes. Right there in the car, we prayed, and she asked Jesus to be the Lord of her life. It was a beautiful day, one I will never forget and one I hope she remembers forever.

A LIFE WORTH SAVING

The Lord always had a hand on my oldest daughter. I remember a time when she was about seven. We were in the craft store Michael's, buying craft items for a project we were doing. She was behind me down the next aisle; and as she turned the corner toward me, she looked up and said to me, "Mom, I know this is really strange and is kind of weird and I really feel funny saying it. But for some reason, I keep thinking, I keep feeling like I have an older sister."

My heart leaped and sank all at the same time. How could she know? I quietly pondered the moment in my heart. No response was given, no response was needed. I just soaked in that moment as she proceeded to tell me how she wished she had an older sibling. I know I will need to share with her someday, but not today.

She has always been sensitive to the Lord. About a year before this, she came to me one morning and told me that while she was reading her Bible, sounds began coming out of her mouth. She told me she was praying. She didn't know what she was saying, but she knew she was praying. My heart leaped again. I explained to her that it sounded like the Holy Spirit, and I encouraged her to continue to allow the Lord to pray through her. *Acts 2:17* reads, *"In the last days, God says, I will pour out my Spirit on all people; your sons and daughters will prophesy, your young men will see visions, your old men will dream dreams."* The Lord was present in her life.

Matthew 19:14

*Let the little children come to me, and do not hinder them,
for the kingdom of heaven belongs to such as these.*

A few years later, we had our second child. Her name is Rebekah. Delivery was quick with this one, and she hasn't slowed down since! When we arrived at the hospital, I was already fully effaced. After delivery, the nurse confided in me. She told me how none of the doctors or nurses could understand how I made it to the hospital. She said these are the babies that are usually born in the car on the way to the hospital! Thank you, Lord, for getting us there!

While I was carrying Rebekah, I was part of a Bible study with a group of women. I talked about how the Lord wanted me to pray for her name and how I felt the Lord wanted me to give my daughter a biblical name. However, the only biblical names I could think of was Mary and Martha. I shared how there was one other name that kept coming to my mind as I prayed, but it wasn't biblical. The name was Rebecca.

I was laughing and saying how Rebecca wasn't even a biblical name. It wasn't even a name in the Bible, so why would God keep putting it in my heart and mind? Well, little did I know the name Rebekah was in the Bible. One of the women look at me puzzled. She proceeded to informed me that there was actually a Rebekah in the Bible. *Proverbs 27:9 (ESV)* reads, *"Oil and perfume make the heart glad, and the sweetness of a friend comes from his earnest counsel."*

I was shocked. I have read the Bible from top to bottom, from Genesis to Revelations, many times; yet a Rebekah never stood out to me. After the Bible study, I went home and spent some time in the Bible looking through to find and read about this Rebecca. Sure enough, she was in there. The spelling was a little different—Rebekah—but it was a beautiful name. Rebekah was the mother of Jacob and Esau.

As I began to read about her, I thought to myself, *This is not good! Lord, what are you trying to say?* She was the one in the Bible who put one child against the other! At home, I prayed. I was led to look up the meaning of Rebekah as I did with Michaela. Rebekah, a rope with a noose. *Well, that's strange*, I thought. "Lord what does that mean?" I began to ask. I began to seek. I continued to research and pray.

The Lord spoke to me, "To tie firmly or to bind. Captivating; beauty."

As I continued to pray, what the Lord began saying to me was she was to be tied firmly to Him. In *Colossians 3:14*, it says, *"And over all these virtues put on love, which binds them all together in perfect unity."* Rebekah is that child—the second born, the one who always seeks peace, always pursues unity. She pulls everyone together, the first to apologize, always striving to get along with everyone. She has a smile that would light up a room, captivating beauty not only on the outside but also beauty from within.

When Rebekah was about five, we were playing a game of Bible land (just like Candy Land except about the Bible). While playing the game, she began asking me more about Jesus. I explained how Jesus died on the cross for her sins and that He loves her very much. She was moved by the Spirit and asked me to pray with her, and she received Jesus as her Lord and Savor that day.

Names mean a lot. There are many times in the Bible that the Lord changed names or had given new names. He changed Abram's name to Abraham in *Genesis 17:1–6* *"because I am making you the ancestor of many nations."* God changed Sarai to Sarah. Under one teaching, we were taught the change to Sarah was to show that God breathed life into Sarah and she was able to bear a son. God told Abraham to name his son Isaac, which means *"I will establish my covenant with him."* God sent an Angel to Zacharia *(Luke 1:13)* and told him his wife would have a son and to give him the name John. In *Matthew 1:21*, it says, The angel of the Lord appeared unto Joseph in a dream, *"She shall bring forth a son and his name shall be Jesus: for he shall save his people from their sins."* Jesus, the most powerful name, means to deliver, to rescue.

Four years later, we had another daughter. Her name is Olivia. We had no idea what to name her. We prayed to the Lord as we did for our other daughters. This time, our daughter's name would come through my husband. We were visiting my brother-in-law, and we began talking about my pregnancy and how we hadn't picked a name. I wanted to name her Miyah; no reason, I just liked it.

My husband, however, wanted her name to mean something. He wasn't keen on the name Miyah. He's a jokester, so the sound of that name always made him laugh. While visiting his brother, he brought up something about olive and how the Bible talks about an olive tree (Noah saw the olive leaf and knew it was safe to exit the arc.) My brother-in-law and my husband began talking back and forth about this olive tree, and suddenly, my husband bursts out the name Olivia.

> *I will be like the dew to Israel; he will blossom like a lily, like a cedar of Lebanon he will send down his roots; his young shoots will grow. His splendor will be like an olive tree, his fragranced liked a cedar of Lebanon. (Hos. 14:5–6)*

I had never even thought of the name before. We looked at each other in awe. I looked up the meaning of Olivia—peace (extending an olive branch). We both knew right away that her name would be Olivia Miyah. I later looked up the meaning of Miyah, and as always, God was faithful. In Hebrew, Miyah means life. It also means "God is my fortress. God is my salvation. God is my stronghold."

We decided to schedule her delivery. It was a week before my due date. My husband was driving a truck at the time and would sometimes deliver in Boston. We didn't live close to family. And with the other two girls at home, I just didn't want to risk it. It was a blessing that we did schedule the birth when we did. It was a dry birth, and during delivery, the cord was wrapped around her neck twice.

Every time I pushed, her heart rate dropped. The doctor told us there was nothing she could do, and I had to push. When she was born, she wasn't breathing. They worked on her for what seemed like hours, yet it was only a matter of minutes. It was so quiet in the room. They took her over to the side of the room, and no one said a word.

I looked over at my husband and asked what was going on. He said nothing. I looked around frantically and began asking why she wasn't crying. Finally, I heard her let out that newborn cry. The cry, as parents, you wait to hear. Miyah—life; Olivia—peace. Thank you, Lord, for your protection and your provision. She is the biggest hugger and animal lover. The smile animals bring to her face brings life and joy.

Olivia asked Jesus into her heart when she was about ten. We read a devotional Bible with her every night in her room when she was little. Looking back, I'm not sure why we stopped. One night, my middle daughter was reading the devotional with her, and it was talking about giving your life to Jesus. Olivia was asking questions, then she said, "I want to do that!"

My daughter came and told me that Olivia was asking a lot of questions, so I went in to talk to her. "What do you what to do?" I asked.

"I want to give my heart to Jesus!" She gave her heart to Jesus that night right there in her room, in her bed. We finished up her devotional, and this momma's heart was full.

Romans 10:9–11 reads, *"Because, if you confess with your mouth that Jesus is Lord and believe in our heart that God raised him from the dead, you will be saved. For with the heart, one believes and is justified, and with the mouth one confesses and is saved."*

I found myself in a conversation with a friend at church. She was pregnant and was struggling to choose a name for her child. She was having a boy, and she was about five months along. She just couldn't decide what to name him. The Lord put it on my heart to share with her what He had spoken to me about names.

I told her how the Lord impressed upon me, while I was pregnant, to pray and seek Him for the name He had already chosen for the life I was carrying. I shared how I was reminded to do so for all my children. I shared with her how He was the one that named the girls. I encouraged her to do the same. When I left, she seemed encouraged to seek Him.

A few weeks went by, maybe a month, and I had heard that she had lost her baby. I was devastated for her and her family. She approached me a few weeks later at church, pulled me aside, and thanked me. She thanked me for encouraging her to seek the Lord for the name of her baby. She shared with me that the name the Lord had given her son was Samuel. After she lost her baby, the Lord put it on her heart to research his name. In the Bible, Samuel was Hannah's son's name. Hannah couldn't conceive, so she prayed to the Lord to have a child.

In *1 Samuel 1:11*, it reads, *"She made a special promise to God and said, 'Lord All-Powerful, you can see how sad I am. Remember me. Don't forget me. If you will give me a son, I will give him to you. He will be yours his whole life.'"* Hannah promised the Lord that if He blessed her with a child, she would give her child back to Him. *First Samuel 1:27* reads, *"I prayed for this child, and the Lord answered my prayer. He gave me this child. And now I give this child to the Lord. He will serve the lord all his life."*

My friend struggled to get pregnant, so this pregnancy had been an answer to prayer and the loss was great. She continued to share with me that by seeking the Lord and asking Him what name He had for her son, He had brought her peace. The name Samuel had given her peace, knowing her child was "given back to the Lord" and he's safe in the arms of Jesus.

The Lord uses us as his hands and feet—to love, to encourage, and to share. We never know the circumstances of what others are going through or will go through. We never know how and what God is going to use in our lives to touch others. Let's be obedient to share. Sharing can be hard. It leaves us wide open. Do it anyway. Our testimonies need to be shared. *First John 5:11* says, *"And this is the testimony: God has given us eternal life, and this life is in his Son."*

Exodus 23:20

See, I am sending an angel ahead of you to guard you along the way and to bring you to the place I have prepared.

We were at the same church for seventeen years. We loved our church and our church family. It was the church we were saved in, married in, and baptized in. When I finally gave birth to our first child, there was no doubt it would be the same church we would dedicate our daughter in. We prayed about dedicating our child to the Lord. It was a faith-filled time for us.

Different churches have different traditions when it comes to babies. The church we attended was a Protestant Church, and it had a fourfold ministry to present who Jesus is.

1. He is our Savior.

> *It is a trustworthy statement, deserving full acceptance, that Christ Jesus came into the world to save sinners, among whom I am foremost of all. (1 Tim. 1:15)*

> *For the Son of Man has come to seek and to save that which was lost. (Luke 19:10)*

> *She will bear a Son; and you shall call His name Jesus, for He will save His people from their sins. (Matt. 1:21)*

2. He is the baptizer of the Holy Spirit.

   Now the Lord is the Spirit, and where the Spirit of the Lord is, there is freedom. (2 Cor. 3:17)

   Do you not know that your bodies are temples of the Holy Spirit, who is in you, whom you have received from God? (1 Cor. 6:19–20)

   But the Advocate, the Holy Spirit, whom the Father will send in my name, will teach you all things and will remind you of everything I have said to you. (John 14:26)

3. He is our healer.

   I will restore your health, and I will heal your wounds, declares the Lord. (Jer. 30:17)

   So, they cried out to the Lord in their distress, and God saved them from their desperate circumstances, God gave the order and healed them. (Psalm 107:19–21)

   If any of you are sick, they should call for the leaders of the church, and the elders should pray over them, anointing them with oil in the name of the Lord. Prayer that comes from faith will heal the sick and will restore them to health. And if they have sinned, they will be forgiven. (James 5:14–15)

4. The coming king.

   Behold, He is coming with the clouds, and every eye will see him, even those who pierced him, and all the tribes of the earth will mourn over Him, so it is to be. Amen. (Rev. 1:7)

A LIFE WORTH SAVING

I kept looking in the night visions, and behold, with the clouds of heaven One like a Son of Man was coming. And He came up to the Ancient of Days and was presented before him. (Dan. 7:13)

There are differences among churches, even churches that believe Jesus is the Son of God, that He died on the cross and rose again, and that He is the one and only true God—Elohim. I was brought up Catholic. I was baptized as a baby, and I made my first communion. When I was sixteen, I made my conformation.

Most Catholics baptize their babies. Some Protestants baptize when the child is old enough to make the decision for themselves. Protestants usually dedicate babies, which is the parent's commitment to raise the child in the Lord with the help of a church family. Dedication is when we pray over our children and commit to raise them to know the Lord. We see this in the Old Testament, in 1 Samuel 1:21–28, when Hannah brought Samuel to the temple. We see it again in the New Testament in Luke 2:22. They brought Jesus to Jerusalem so that they could present him to the Lord.

To dedicate means to devote your time and your effort to something. To dedicate to the Lord is to make a commitment to God that you will teach your children about Him. Usually, what happens at a dedication is the congregation will pray as a church over the child and over the family. It is the parents who are making the decision to raise their child in the Lord, and the congregation is praying in agreement that they too will help raise the child to know God.

Baptism is the outward expression of the repentance of sin. It is done when people recognized their sin and want to be washed clean and start new. In *Acts 2:38*, it says, *"And Peter said to them, 'Repent and be baptized every one of you in the name of Jesus Christ for the forgiveness of your sins, and you will receive the gift of the Holy Spirit.'"* The water symbolically washes your sins away. *Acts 22:16* says, *"And now why do you wait? Rise and be baptized and wash away your sins, calling on his name."*

Our sins are washed and covered by the blood of Jesus. In our first home, when we were first married, I bought a wall hanging that read, *"'Come now, let us settle the matter,' says the Lord. 'Though your sins are like scarlet, they shall be as white as snow; though they are red as crimson, they shall be like wool'" (Isa. 1:18).* I placed it in our recently remodeled bathroom. It was such a powerful scripture to remind me every day of how much the Lord loves me and how much He had done for me over the years.

After my first daughter was born, we set a date to have her dedication. Michaela, "who is like the Lord," was the name given to her. As the time grew closer, I was getting extremely anxious. I felt like I had no idea how to raise a daughter, never mind how to raise her to know the Lord. Neither of our families had taken this path, so we were the first.

I began to pray. I prayed for the Lord to give me wisdom, and to guide me. I prayed that the Lord would be there and be present at the dedication as well as in the rest of our lives. I knew I could not do it alone. I prayed that my Father would be there, my heavenly Father. My earthly "fathers" would not be there. However, I had someone greater, Abba Father. He was always there for me, and I prayed in expectation knowing that He would be there on that day for all of us.

He would not fail me. I went into that day full of excitement, full of anticipation, knowing the Lord heard my prayers and would meet me. He would meet us right where we were. While we were on the platform with our little girl being prayed over, I felt His presence; He was there. I sensed His presence around us the entire time. However, when we walked off the platform, I felt like there was something missing. I don't know why I felt that way. I know He is faithful, I know He heard my prayers, I know He was there, I felt His presence; so what was it?

I have seen angels before but just once. It was during a worship service on a Sunday morning. I remember worshipping with all my being, and while worshipping, I looked up toward heaven. As I looked up, I could see what seemed like the heavens begin to open. I could see angels of the Lord descending between the clouds, and they were hovering above us. It was like they were all around us.

As I continued to worship, I looked up toward heaven again, and I could see that some were singing and some were praying. It was like the heavens opened up, and we all joined together in worship in the heavenly realms. It was beautiful. I share this because a week after Michaela's dedication, a man from our church, who I did not know very well, approached me. He asked if our daughter was the one that was dedicated the week before. I smiled and told him that yes, indeed, that was our daughter.

He proceeded to tell me that he was supposed to come and share something with us last week, but he had been too nervous. I could still sense his nervousness as he spoke. He shared that when he left church the previous week, the Lord would not leave him alone. When he got home that Sunday, the Lord continued to speak to him about what he saw at the dedication. The Lord continued to press upon him to go and speak of what he saw.

He continued, "Last week during your daughter's dedication, I could sense the presence of the Lord. I looked up at the three of you, and I saw an angel of the Lord descending from heaven. The angel of the Lord hovered over your daughter, over all of you. Its arms spread wide, and its wings surrounded, encircled all of you and the glory of the Lord shown all around." My husband immediately looked at me, wide-eyed. He had known my prayers. He had known that I had prayed for the presence of the Lord to be there. He knew just how much it meant to me to hear that the Lord was there and what the Lord had done for me, for us on that day. My Father was present. My husband stood quietly, knowing the Lord had again answered my prayers.

> *He will cover you with His feathers and under His wings you will take refuge; His faithfulness will be your shield and rampart."* A little further in verses 11–16, it continues, *For He will command His angels concerning you to guard you in all your ways. They will lift you up in their hands, so that you will not strike your foot against a stone. You will tread on the lion and the cobra; you will trample the great lion and the serpent. "Because He loves me," says the lord, "I will rescue him; I will protect him, for he acknowledges my name. He will*

call on me, and I will answer him; I will be with him in trouble, I will deliver him and honor him, with long life I will satisfy him and show him my salvation. (Psalms 91:4, 9–16)

The Lord answered my prayers that day, like He always does. He's going to take care of her. He's going to take care of us. I had to put my trust and faith in Him. He sent an angel of the Lord down to earth that day to be with us. He heard our prayers, and He responded. He gave a man a vision. *Acts 2:17* reads, *"In the last days, God says, I will pour out my Spirit on all people. Your sons and daughters will prophesy, your young men will see visions, your old men will dream dreams."* He will cover me; He will cover her. We will take refuge in him.

Exodus 23:20 says, *"See, I am sending an angel ahead of you to guard you along the way and to bring you to the place I have prepared."*

The Lord is always present. The Lord hears. The Lord listens. The Lord speaks.

He is always faithful.

1 Peter 3:15

But in your hearts revere Christ as Lord. Always be prepared to give an answer to everyone who asks you to give the reason for the hope that you have. But do this with gentleness and respect.

After I had my second child, the Lord opened the door for me to go back to school. I signed up at a local community college and began to take classes. This is where I was able to share a little bit of my faith and some of what the Lord had already done in my life. Public speaking class was on the agenda, and I was terrified! Public speaking wasn't something I was ever comfortable with, but I knew the Lord was in it. He would give me the strength I needed, and He would see me through.

In my public speaking class, we were asked to pick different topics based on the teacher's leading. The first topic we were to write about was something that would be informative. I chose to write my first paper about Christianity. My teacher gave me a little bit of a pushback on it. She said there was nothing I could share that hadn't already been shared. God, however, had placed some students in the class that always seemed to respectfully question the teacher as to why she didn't want me to speak on a specific subject.

One student raised his hand and questioned why it was okay for another classmate to speak on a different religion, but it wasn't okay for me to speak on Christianity. After my teacher was confronted by another student, she agreed to allow me to proceed with my paper but on one condition. She didn't want to hear all the same old stuff used to "share the gospel." She wanted to make sure that it would be different and informative. I took on the challenge. I was excited to speak on something that was so personal and close to my heart.

I titled my first paper "The Bread, the Cup and the Cross." It was a privilege to present my faith to the class. I shared how the cup represented Jesus's blood, the blood that He shed on the cross for us that covered our sins. In order for us to be in right relationship with God the Father, we had to be without sin. Which is impossible. That's why we needed Jesus to be our sacrificial Lamb.

I shared that in the Old Testament, a spotless lamb had to be brought to the altar every year to be sacrificed for the sins of each family. There was no forgiveness without the shedding of blood. The blood is what covers our sins. The bread represents His broken body, the body He chose to give up and to be broken in our place. He chose the will of His father and took on all of our sins, the sins of the whole world, so we would have hope for eternity. He chose to take on that kind of punishment for us. The cross represents Christ's victory over sin and death. He is no longer there. He has risen. All who put their hope in the bread, cup, and the cross will live life eternally with the Creator. The Father sees us through Jesus's blood. The blood washes our sins away.

After I presented my paper to the class, my teacher informed me that she had a brother who was a Christian. She told me she had never heard the gospel explained like that. God moved. What struck her the most was the correlation between the Old Testament and the New Testament and the importance of the shedding of blood to cover our sins. Jesus's blood, shed on the cross (New Testament), was needed for the covering of our sin; and it replaced the need (in the Old Testament) to sacrifice a spotless lamb on the altar once a year for the forgiveness of our sins. Jesus did it once and for all. It is finished. *John 19:30* says, *"It is finished!" And bowing His head, He gave up His spirit."*

She was perplexed. She asked if I had gone to seminary school. I was surprised by her question as I answered no. She asked how I knew all the information that was shared without going to seminary. I smiled and told her I didn't know nearly as much as someone who went to seminary. I did encourage her, however, to open the Bible, pray, and read it. I shared with her how God will reveal anything and everything she's ever wanted or needed to know. It's all written in the Bible, and He was willing and waiting to answer any question she had.

Matthew 7:7 says, *"Ask and it will be given to you, seek and you will find, knock and the door will be opened to you."*

As Christians, we forget that the simple truths we know and have learned are not simple truths to everyone. If we don't tell them, how will they know? Open up, pray, and be ready to give an account for what you believe. *First Peter 3:15* reads, *"But in your hearts revere Christ as Lord. Always be prepared to give an answer to everyone who asks you to give the reason for the hope that you have. But do this with gentleness and respect."* That's what we are here for. I'm praying that someday, she will seek the Lord. I know when she does, God will be faithful to her. *Psalms 145:18* says, *"The Lord is near to all who call on him, to all who call on him in truth."*

The next paper we had to write had to be controversial. I was extremely nervous, but I believed the Lord wanted me to speak on my abortion. I prayed. When it was my turn to share my topic, my teacher flat out told me no. She told me she would not let me do my paper on abortion. Again, there was a classmate who spoke up and asked her why she wouldn't allow me to do my paper on that specific topic.

They again reminded her that we were supposed to pick controversial subjects; that's what the class was about. She told the class it was because she already knew where I stood on it, so there was no point in me speaking on it. She wanted me to choose a different topic. A few students suggested I speak to her after class while others suggested I just pick another subject. I sat quietly for the rest of the class and prayed.

At the end of class, I felt led to go up to the front of class to talk to her before I left. She explained to me that she didn't think I had the right to speak about something I knew nothing about. I looked around the room and noticed that there were a few students who hadn't left yet. The Lord prompted me, and I opened my mouth and asked her quietly, "What if I told you I have had an abortion?" I paused and continued quietly, "Would that change your mind?" She looked up at me slowly, looked me in the eye, and shook her head yes.

The door was open, and I took a deep breath. I went home and prayed and prepared. With the grace and the love of the Lord, I was able to share with the class all that had happened in that part of my life. I was led by the Lord to bring in and to show photos and ultrasounds of my two babies, the ones that survived. I was able to share and show what those babies looked like in an ultrasound at ten weeks as well as twenty weeks. I brought pictures of what they looked like now, one that was two and the other who was five.

What a powerful message, one only the Lord could have put together. I showed and shared how these two beautiful babies that I didn't deserve but that I was blessed with were the two babies that survived. I was then able to share about the one that never had the privilege of taking her first breath on this side of heaven, the child of mine that did not survive here on earth. I shared hope. I shared how my baby girl is in the arms of Jesus. I would see her someday.

He does not treat us as our sins deserve or repay us according to our iniquities. (Psalm 103:10)

If we confess our sins, he is faithful and just to forgive us our sins, and to cleanse us from all unrighteousness. (1 John 1:19)

Here's an excerpt from the paper I wrote.

In 1987, a 16-year-old girl enters an abortion clinic. As she sits across the table from her counselor, she struggles to hold back her tears. She is almost 12 weeks pregnant and the thought of ending this pregnancy is overwhelming. When she learned of her pregnancy abortion never even entered her mind. Yet here she sits wondering, "How did I get here." The counselor noticing her struggles blurts out, it's okay it's not a baby anyway.

1987 Abortion clinics told people that an embryo was not a baby until 12 wks into pregnancy. Today when asked if the baby is a human being, they refuse to define it. Women are choosing to have abortions based on misinformation or lack thereof.

1964 planned parenthood published a pamphlet promoting "birth control" when asked if the pill was an abortion they answered, "Definity not. An abortion kills the life of a baby after it has already begun."

At 2 weeks the baby already has 46 chromes. which predetermine the baby's physical characteristics including Eye/hair color.

At 3 weeks the backbone, spinal column, nervous system is forming. Kidneys, liver, and intestines are taking shape.

At 5 weeks the heart has begun beating. neural tube enlarges into three parts soon to be the brain. The spinal cord has the appearance of a tail.

7 weeks facial features are visible including mouth and tongue. Eyes have a retina. Major nervous systems are developed. The baby has its own blood type distinct from the mothers.

8 weeks arms and legs have lengthened, and fingers can be seen. Brain waves can be measured.

10 weeks heart is almost completely developed. Bypass valves divert the blood away from the lungs. 20 tiny baby teeth are forming in the gums.

12 weeks vocal cords complete. Child can and does sometimes cry. Brain is fully formed. The child can feel pain.

I pray and believe that the young students in that class were touched, not by me but by the Lord that day. The Lord uses all our experiences, good and bad, to speak truth, light, and love to others. There is always hope; there is always forgiveness. A few years later, my husband went back to school to be a teacher, and guess who he had for a public speaking teacher? The same teacher I had years before.

As he talked about his family in class one day, she looked up at him and realized who I was. She said to him, "I think I know who your wife is. I may have had her in class." I pray and believe that a seed was planted, and someday, she will come to know the Lord Jesus Christ as her Lord and Savior. Never be ashamed of the gospel of Christ. Share. Allow the Lord to speak through you, and the Lord will do what He does. Never be afraid to speak the truth in love and leave the rest up to the Lord.

Genesis 2:24

This is why a man leaves his father and mother and is united with his wife, and they become one flesh.

After my first daughter was born, we had family over to meet and to celebrate her birth. One family member who had been pregnant around the same time had just had a miscarriage. When she arrived, she sat in the corner. She didn't come near me or the baby. With all she was going through, her reaction was understandable. Her loss was too great. About a year went by, and she was finally able to conceive and carry her baby to full term. She had a daughter. She was born healthy, and everyone rejoiced.

As the years went on, she had a few more miscarriages and was not able to have another child. I was able to conceive again, and I had my second daughter. As her grief took over, hurt and resentment seemed to grow. There never really was time to rejoice. Her struggle and losses were so great that it overshadowed the joy we had for our newest member of the family.

She began to share with others how she couldn't understand why I was able to have another child. How was I able to have another child when she was not? She shared her feelings with family members and close friends. When I heard of all that was being said, I was brought back to the place, a place from long ago. The Lord had brought me so far; and yet in one instant, in one single moment, I was quickly brought back and began to believe the lie of the enemy again. The lie that I wasn't washed clean by His blood and that I was still unworthy, that I wasn't forgiven.

In my heart, all that I felt as a child came flooding back. I was hurt by the comments that were made, yet I couldn't say anything. Even though I was hurt, I could understand her pain, her loss, and her grief. However, part of our joy was taken away, stolen. We weren't fully able to rejoice and be glad. Every time we were around family, there was a cloud of resentment, hurt, and anger.

As time went by, the divide grew. The hurt from my childhood now compounded in adulthood. Hearing how I didn't deserve to have another child; how I was not good enough, how my husband wasn't a good enough father, and how her husband was a better father than mine ever would be was hurtful. It seemed like I should have never been afforded the grace and forgiveness the Lord had bestowed upon me.

It's hard to see or understand that God is a God of forgiveness, grace, and mercy. It was hard to see when, in that moment, you're not feeling it for yourself.

I tried so hard for our family to be close. It's what I always wanted, but no matter how hard I tried, I always felt the door was shut. If I wanted just us moms to go out to lunch on a Mother's Day or to have a girl's shopping day, it was always met with negativity. It was hard to see my girls trying and wanting sleepovers and hangouts that never would come. We just couldn't break through. We were always held at arm's length.

The negative comments toward me would continue for years. In the mists of joy, in the mists of our blessings, there are always others that struggle. It's human to have these struggles in life, but if held on to too tightly and not dealt with, they linger and begin to fester. They bring resentment. *Hebrews 12:15* says, *"See to it that no one falls short of the grace of God; that no bitter root grows up to cause trouble, and defile many."*

It can steal the blessings. That's what happened to me. I was never allowed to fully enjoy the blessings. I was never allowed to fully rejoice in my children. I was never allowed to speak of my children, of their accomplishments or their struggles. I was ignored and put down. When we would try to get together, to shop, or to see Christmas lights or have sleepovers, it was always a no. The reason given, I had too many children. I had been blessed with three beautiful children that I didn't deserve. What really do any of us deserve?

There came a time in my life that the hurt had become so deep, I had to stop seeing my family for a while. I was always told that we needed to stick together because we only had each other. I felt a huge burden to continue to show up. I always felt a need to please. I was still that little girl that couldn't do anything right. I remember trying to reach out and have conversations. They would always end in arguments. I was told I was always starting trouble. It was painful. It became uncomfortable to even step foot into the house. There was so much hurt, so much unforgiveness in such a small family.

We headed to my mom's house one particular holiday. I was so full of anxiety that I was in tears. The whole way there, I cried. I hated knowing that all my anxieties were brought on at the thought of visiting family. It was always the same. I knew I was going to walk through that door and be ignored. I was anticipating all the stuff I was going to endure. I talked through my tears the entire ride. I told my husband how I just didn't know what to do any more.

No matter what I did, it was wrong. I will walk through the door, and they will already be mad. No matter what gift I give, they will make fun of it. Nothing was ever good enough. I was never good enough. My husband listened to me as he drove. By the time we got to the house, I was a mess. My husband stopped the car and parked in front of the house, and I continued to sob. We sat there, my husband in the driver's seat and my two little kids in the back. They were too young to understand, or so I hoped.

My husband, who had been quiet the whole time just listening, turned and looked at me. "You can't do this anymore."

I was a little surprised, "Can't do what? I can't cry and be upset? Well, I am!"

He explained "No. I mean this is not healthy for you and it's not going to be healthy for our girls. This is not healthy for our family."

I stopped and looked at him. "What are you saying?" I asked.

His reply, "We need to stop coming."

I was even more upset. I shot back, "I can't do that. That's my family. It's only the three of us, and I can't leave too."

He just looked at me. "We can't do this anymore. It is not healthy." I looked at him shocked. I cleaned my face, and we went inside.

Tension, comments, ignoring—all the same. I was uncomfortable. I remember that year trying to buy something special, like I tried to every year. I tried so hard to get something they would love. They never did. "Why would you buy me this? Why would I want something like that?" These were some of the comments I would get.

I left that day and began to seek the Lord. Over the next few days during my devotional time, I continued to seek the Lord. *Was this unhealthy? Was I unhealthy? Was it okay to stop going?* I had lived this for so long and felt like this for so long, I didn't even know what was right anymore. To me, this was normal. I continued to seek the Lord every morning for healing and direction. The Lord brought me to Genesis 2:24, *"This is why a man leaves his father and mother and is united with his wife, and they become one flesh."*

This is written and is used in marriages all the time. On this day, the Lord opened my eyes to the deeper spiritual meaning of this scripture. Emotionally, I was still very much connected to my family. Which you might say was okay, maybe even normal, but the Lord showed me that to the point I had gotten was not healthy. It had become a codependent relationship. Maybe it had always been.

I was putting my relationship with my family above my marriage relationship. Above my children. I was trying to make everyone happy at the expense of my new family. I was allowing the toxins from my childhood to seep into my relationship with my husband, and eventually, it would seep into my children's lives. The Lord was saying I needed to leave my "father and mother's house" emotionally and, for a time, physically. It was time to leave and cleave to my husband. I needed to hear him, I needed to listen to him, and yes, I needed to obey him.

Obey is such a hard word for some of us. In some cases, it should be when the word *obey* isn't used in a biblical content. This was, and I needed to listen. I wasn't obeying blindly; I was taking what my husband said and bringing it to the Lord. I had a hard time with the thought of walking away, even for a little bit. Was the information my husband was giving me from the Lord? It was. The Lord gave me a new revelation of a familiar scripture. I knew he was right.

My husband was speaking wisdom into the situation, and I needed to listen as hard as it was. I needed some time. I needed to move forward with my own healing. Healing needed to take place in me. Powerful. It was powerful. *Psalms 147:3* reads, *"He heals the brokenhearted and binds up their wounds."* Whenever you seek the Lord and He speaks, it's always powerful. The Lord shared with me that He wanted me to take this time to heal. I was awestruck. *Me? You want to heal me?* I needed to make that phone call and explain that I need to take some time. But how? I began to seek and ask the Lord to guide my conversation. I didn't want to hurt anyone, and the Lord didn't want me to hurt anymore. "Oh Lord," I cried out. "What should I say?"

Not everyone understands when you're walking with the Lord, and He begins to do things in your life that others may not understand. But sometimes, those tough things need to happen because He wants to heal us. He wants to put us back together. He reveals things that sometimes may upset the apple cart, but there is a shaking that needs to take place for things to fall into a healthy place.

Hebrews 12:27 reads, *"The words 'once more' indicate the removing of what can be shaken—that is, created things—so that what cannot be shaken will remain."*

The next step would be difficult. Making this phone call would be one of them. How could I communicate this effectively? I again continued to pray. Well actually, I began to complain a bit. I told Him all the things He already knew. He listened and let me get some things off my chest. "Lord, I have to stop going over there because of them. The things they have said and done have been so hurtful!"

The Lord suddenly stopped me right in the middle of my thoughts. Quietly, He said, "No, it's not about them. It is about you. It is about your healing. You need time to heal." Sigh. When the Lord speaks, it's simple. He brought peace to my soul. "Tell them, 'I need time to heal.'"

As beautiful as it sounded from Jesus, when you feel as though you have been blamed for everything your entire life, the last thing you want to do is say "it's me." You feel like you need to fight and defend yourself. But the Lord gave me peace—Shalom—a peace that was so deep and so beautiful. I made that phone call. There was no blame involved, and the conversation went smoothly. God is good. It seemed to have been received well when I explained that I was the one that needed to heal.

Unfortunately, not long after the phone call, I received a letter in the mail from an extended family member. This letter was not kind. It was full of reasons why I was a horrible Christian. I was told I was an awful person and an awful daughter. What kind of daughter takes her children away from their own family? That was pretty much what was written. So many things, so many emotions.

This woman was a Christian. We didn't know each other well at all. As hard as it was for me to go through this, I knew the Lord was with me. I knew that was not what I was doing. How did this woman even know? How did she even get my address? No answer, no response was required. It was time to heal. *Phil. 4:7* says, *"And the peace of God, which transcends all understanding, will guard your hearts and your minds in Christ Jesus."*

It was time to separate my childhood from my adulthood. It was time for me to accept who I was as a wife and a mother. I was learning that my new family has now become my nuclear family. I still loved my family, and they would still be part of my life. They were still a part of my family. I was the one who needed to adjust that relationship to get a healthy perspective from the Lord.

I would say it was about a year, maybe a little more, before we rejoined the family. During that time, the Lord really showed me His love, and He taught me to forgive. What the Lord showed me was as much as I was broken, they were broken too. Right or wrong, they were hurting too. They were doing what they could to survive. No parent is ever going to be perfect, least of all me.

The Lord brought me to a place of freedom. He taught me forgiveness, and He brought me through to healing. When I returned, I was whole. Our relationship began to develop into what it should have been all along, a mutual respect and understanding that only the Lord could have given. I read something the other day: "Broken things can become blessed things if you let God do the mending." *Psalm 34:18–19* says, *"The Lord is close to the broken hearted; saves those who are discouraged. A righteous man may have many troubles, but the Lord delivers him from them all."*

Isaiah 43:18–19

Forget the former things; do not dwell on the past.
See, I am doing a new thing! Now it springs up;
do you not perceive it? I am making a way in
the wilderness and streams in the wastelands.

Four years later, I was pregnant with my last child. I wondered, *Lord, this time, if it's your will, I'm open and ready to have a boy.* I began to prepare my heart.

While I was carrying my last child, I began to process what it would be like to have a boy, a son. I didn't grow up around boys or men, so I had no idea how to raise them. Yet I began to have this tug. I began to speak to the Lord, "If it is your will, let it be done."

As I would walk through stores, I would notice all the little boy things—clothing, toys, shoes—and I would wonder, *Lord, this time, I think I'm ready.* I began to feel a little bit of joy in expectation. I began to settle in my heart the idea of having a boy. I thought to myself, *My husband would be blessed to have a son.*

About five months later, we entered the ultrasound room together, I readied myself. When the results came through, they showed that we were having another healthy baby girl. When we left the room, I found myself overwhelmed with emotions. I found the closest seat and sat down.

My husband, concerned, stopped, sat down next to me and asked, "What's wrong? Are you okay?"

Thoughts began to flood my mind. I was happy and relieved to hear that we were having a heathy baby girl, but emotions began to overwhelm me. I turned and looked at him and began to apologize. He looked at me puzzled. "Why are you apologizing to me?"

I looked down and back up again. "I'm sorry. I'm not able to give you a son."

The words of the past came flooding back to me. "Your father wanted a son."

I looked up. "Don't you want a son?"

He replied, "No, it's never been important to me."

As I sat in the waiting room, the truth was realized. The former things no longer applied. The Lord was doing a new thing. He was making a way for me out of the wilderness and out of the wastelands. The thoughts and beliefs of the past no longer applied.

Isaiah 43:18–19 says, *"Forget the former things; do not dwell on the past. See, I am doing a new thing! Now it springs up; do you not perceive it? I am making a way in the wilderness and streams in the wastelands."*

Chains had been broken, and I had been set free. Isaiah 54:17 says, *"'No weapon forged against you will prevail, and you will refute every tongue that accuses you. This is the heritage of the servants of the Lord, and this is their vindication from me,' declares the Lord."*

Matthew 23:26

—⚉—

You blind Pharisee, first clean the inside of the cup and of the dish, so that the outside of it may become clean also.

When we began looking for houses, we looked in the town I wanted to live in. The town where I grew up. The town I always wanted to raise my children. Unfortunately, the prices were too high. Some would say to me, "Where is your faith? Don't you believe God will provide?" I had faith. However, sometimes, what we want is not what the Lord wants for us.

While praying and speaking to my husband, he felt a lot of pressure. Can we afford it? We needed to make sure we could afford the basics. If we couldn't, how would that be responsible? We wanted a house we could afford, something we could afford on one salary. I wanted the option to be able to stay at home with the kids when they were little. We also wanted the option to send them to a private Christian school.

The plan was, I could work and pay for private school. We wanted them to have every opportunity to get to know the Lord and grow in him. I needed it for myself just as much. I knew I would need the help. We could not find a house in the area we wanted that we could afford. It was frustrating. We eventually found a house we could afford on one salary; it was just a few towns over.

Honestly, it was a dump. I remember our realtor saying, "I usually work with clients who have champagne taste on a beer budget." We laughed. We were going in the complete opposite direction. We went for the least expensive we could find. We did and still do try to be as responsible as we can with our money. That is good practice; however, there may be a false sense of humility mixed in there with a little bit of low self-esteem.

I think I believed deep down inside that it's really all I'm/we were worth. Anyone else ever feel like that? It's something I sometimes still find myself struggling with to this day. I remember going out to dinner to celebrate the purchase of our "new" house. The entire time, I held back tears because I felt like I was letting go of a dream. I wanted to be surrounded by the people I grew up with spiritually, and I wanted that for my children. No matter how many houses we looked at, nothing in that area worked.

It was our daughter's first birthday, and we invited everyone over to celebrate. The house was still a work in progress. A big work in progress. While I was giving a tour to one of our guests, I'll use the term lightly, the house was under one thousand square feet, she asked me why we were working on the inside of the house before the outside. The outside had old clapboard and the paint was pealing; it was not very appealing.

As we continued to walk through the house, I pointed out the different things we had been working on. When I say *we*, I really mean my husband. I always had the vision, but he was the one who would take up the task. As we walked around the house, I began to share with her something the Lord had put on my heart: "God works from the inside out." It's kind of like what we were before we met Jesus. We can do all we can to make the outside of ourselves look beautiful, but if our insides are struggling, it's all for nothing.

Jesus takes our broken pieces and begins to mold them, heal them, and make them into something beautiful, the beauty the Lord created in us before the world even began. The beauty that only comes through His Holy Spirit working in and through us. *First Peter 3:4* says, *"Your beauty should not come from outward adornment, such as elaborate hairstyles and the wearing of gold jewelry or fine clothes. Rather, it should be that of your inner self, the unfading beauty of a gentle and quiet spirit, which is of great worth in God's sight."* When we willingly lay down ourselves before him, that is when he is able to work in us. That is what the Lord had begun to show me through this house process.

As we redid that house, the Lord spoke to me about a lot of things. Most importantly, prayer. I found myself seeking God for my healing and for my growth, but I was learning to pray for others, my town, and my family. That house ended up being my favorite house. I loved that house. The work, the time, and the prayer that went into that house, that went into that time of our lives, was precious.

As we lived and remodeled the house, the Lord put on my heart *Proverbs 22:6, "Train up a child in the way they should go, and even when they are old, they will not turn from it."* My husband gutted that entire house. He added hallways and doorways to make more rooms, and he created built-ins where closets used to be. As rooms were completed, the Lord began to speak to me about learning calligraphy and drawing scripture "around the doorframes."

> *Fix these words of mine in your hearts and minds; tie them as symbols on your head and bind them on your foreheads. Teach them to your children, talking about them when you sit at home and when you walk along the road, when you lie down and when you get up. Write them on the doorframes of your houses and on your gates, so that your days and the days of your children may be many in the land the Lord swore to give your ancestors, as many as the days that the heavens are above the earth. If you carefully observe all these commands, I am giving you to follow—to love the Lord your God to walk in obedience to him and to hold fast to him. (Deut. 11:18–22)*

As the Lord began to lay on my heart this new hobby, I went out and purchased the tools I needed and began to practice. The first scripture was written on the new built-in hutch my husband built in our dining room. We took care of that house from the inside out.

We had a big beautiful tree in the front yard. In the fall, that tree would shed its colorful leaves. We would watch as the two oldest girls played in the leaves. I have a picture of them under that tree, playing in the leaves, that I will treasure forever.

In the back, my husband created a play area with a sandbox and a swing set he put together for the girls. There was also a small garden in the back/side of the house where we planted veggies. It was all so simple, and the presence of the Lord was there. Everything in that house was done in love. Every room was dedicated to the Lord, and every walk I took was filled with silent prayer for that little town and the people in it.

As I shared what the Lord had been doing and speaking to me about raising our children and the importance of writing and applying scriptures in our lives, the pastor's wife approached me and asked if I would be willing to put together a breakout session for a women's conference that our church was hosting. I was shocked and a little nervous. It always seems that when the Lord is teaching me something or bringing me through something, He opens the door and gives an opportunity to share. He wants us to use our stories to encourage others. After a lot of prayer, I submitted to the will of the Father and prepared for the conference.

Proverbs 11:24–25 ESV

One gives freely yet grows all the richer; another withholds what he should give, and only suffers want. Whoever brings blessing will be enriched, and one who waters will himself be watered.

There were tough times when we bought our first home, but the Lord always provided. We were still in the process of fixing the house when my husband was laid off from his job. We were praying and praying for the Lord to open a door for him, like he had so many times before. He eventually did get a job but not one he really liked or wanted, but it was one we needed.

After my first daughter was born, my husband was laid off again. It seemed with every blessing came struggle. Things were getting tough, and we needed some help. I started praying for a job to fill in the gaps. I didn't really know how I would do it with a newborn baby. How would I find a job that would pay enough and still be able to cover childcare?

Childcare was not something I had ever wanted. I wanted to be able to be a stay-at-home mom. As both of us began to pray and seek the Lord, He began to speak. As I was going through my day, the Lord kept putting on my heart "house cleaning." I began to question God. "Lord, is that all I can do? Is that all I am capable of?" I always seem to see myself from this brokenness of my worth. I struggled, feeling like I wasn't worth anything. I, like some of us, seem to carry this baggage from our childhood. We carry it into our adult lives and into our relationships. Even our relationship with God. Will I ever be healed of that? *Philippians 1:6* reads, *"Being confident of this, that he*

A LIFE WORTH SAVING

who began a good work in you will carry it on to completion until the day of Christ Jesus."

The Lord was persistent. Every time I prayed, "house cleaning" would come to my mind. Finally, I relented and started looking in the papers for a cleaning job. Nothing. I couldn't find anything that would pay me what we needed, never mind enough money for childcare. I thought maybe I could take her with me. I continued to pray.

A couple weeks later, while we were at church, a woman who was leading a Bible study we were a part of walked over to me. She started to share how she had been praying and the Lord put me on her heart. She shared how she had been looking for a cleaner for her house and asked if I would be willing to clean for her once a week. I just looked at her in awe. I told her how the Lord had been speaking to me about that; however, I had no experience and I had my daughter to consider.

She laughed and told me she would teach me how she wanted it to be done and she told me I could bring my daughter. She asked if I had a baby swing. That one move of the Lord brought me to start my own cleaning company that lasted for seventeen years. The business continued to grow. I had a friend who worked at a daycare, and when I told her what the Lord was doing, she informed me that her parents were always telling her how they struggle to keep their houses clean because they worked so much! I made up some business cards, and she posted them at work. My cleaning business took off. The Lord took something that made me feel worthless and turned it into something I never could have imagined. He is faithful!

My husband and I were still praying about his situation as well. He had been looking for a more permanent job. He was working, but we were still struggling. We were on a strict budget, and there were some school loans that would be coming due. It was the end of the week, and I had given my husband his budgeted fifteen dollars a week for gas money. Can you even remember gas at that price?

He left to get gas before he headed to his part-time job. When he returned home, he seemed to be pacing and a bit nervous. He shared with me how he saw a homeless man in the parking lot, and he felt like the Lord wanted him to give him the fifteen dollars he had in his pocket. I got extremely nervous and asked if he had given it to him. He told me he didn't but that he really felt like he should have.

I started to cry, and I reminded him that's all we had for gas money. I felt a tug though and told him if he really felt God was telling him to give him the money, then he should go back and do it. He wasn't sure if the man would still be there, but he drove back anyway in obedience. As he turned into the parking lot, he noticed the man was still there. He drove over to him, and he gave him the money and drove away.

The next day he received a call about a job working for a church we had visited a while back. It was a cleaning job on weekends, and it paid $150 a week. That may not sound like a lot to you, but it was an answer to prayer for us. Out of his act of obedience, by giving our last fifteen dollars, the Lord had blessed us tenfold. A few weeks later, my husband received another phone call, this time from a mentor at our church offering him a full-time job working nights with good pay and benefits. That job provided for our family for ten years.

Whoever is generous to the poor lends to the Lord, and he will repay him for his deed. (Proverbs 19:17 ESV)

1 Kings 19:11–13

The Lord said, "Go out and stand on the mountain in the presence of the Lord, for the Lord is about to pass by." Then a great and powerful wind tore the mountains apart and shattered the rocks before the Lord, but the lord was not in the wind. After the wind there was an earthquake, but the Lord was not in the earthquake. After the earthquake came a fire, but the Lord was not in the fire. And after the fire came a gentle whisper. When Elijah heard it, he pulled his cloak over his face and went out and stood at the mouth of the cave.

When my oldest daughter was about three-and-a-half years old, we decided to sign her up for dance class. In the church we attended, there was a group of women that were part of a worship dance team. I loved to watch them worship freely. It was stunning.

While we looked around to find a dance class, I envisioned the women dancing before the Lord at church. There wasn't a dance class around us that really resonated within me. *How can you bring dance class together with worship?* I thought to myself. That's what I was really looking for. I soon found myself in a conversation with friends, sharing, contemplating about a dance class that would bring the two together.

To my pleasant surprise, I was informed about a Christian dance class that was on a Saturday morning. I was excited to hear about it. This would be a great place for my daughter to go! As we talked more, I realized it was a bit of a distance from me, about forty-five minutes away. However, it being on a Saturday, I thought it would be worth the trip. My husband didn't think it was such a good idea because of the distance, but I felt it would be beneficial for her to learn from someone who had a background in worship, not just dance.

I would be the one commuting with her, so I signed her up. Every Saturday morning, I would get up and get the two girls ready, and we would drive my oldest to dance class. I loved it. She loved it. The class would start with scripture reading and prayer. The dance they were performing was a story out of the Bible, and the costumes were beautiful. I loved that the dance studio taught about the Lord as well as danced to honor him. It was worth the trip.

Late one morning, while I was driving home from dance practice, I was in an accident. I was about twenty minutes from home when it happened. I remember looking to my right and seeing the gazebo. This indicated that I was almost home and my turn was coming soon. It was a beautiful morning.

As I drove, we listened to Christian music quietly playing in the background. We were just enjoying a beautiful Saturday morning when suddenly, out of nowhere, I saw black. Everything happened in an instant. I immediately went to put my foot on the break; but as I did, I could hear a quiet voice say, "Take your foot off the break."

As I'm processing this voice, I hear myself start to argue, "Take my foot off the break? That's crazy! It doesn't make sense! I am going to hit that car!" So instead of obeying the still small voice of the Lord, I pushed down on the break even harder. I pushed so hard I could feel my heel hit the floor of the car. I wish I could say in that moment I just trusted and obeyed God without question, but I didn't. Someday, I hope I can learn to hear and recognize God's voice right away and obey. Are you with me? Are you there yet? I'm still working on it. We can only see what is right in front of us; God sees the whole picture.

"Take your foot off the break." I held on tighter to that steering wheel, and as I saw myself getting closer to the blackness, I push down even harder on the break. We made impact. Slowly, as though in slow motion, my car began to spin. I remember looking back calmly at my two girls as we continued to spin. "It's going to be okay.

A LIFE WORTH SAVING

Just hang on we are all going to be okay," I reassured them. The car began to fill with particles and smoke.

As I reflect on that moment in time, let me share something I wrote for that speech class I had to take in college. It went something like this.

> As I enjoyed a peaceful drive on a quiet Saturday afternoon, I could smell the cool crisp January air. Ahead of me I see the clear black pavement moving underneath my wheels and I see the sun warming the ice-covered trees. Out of nowhere, all I see is black. My quiet peaceful drive had just begun to change. In an instant, all at once, everything changed. As blackness flashed in front of my eyes, I quickly pressed my foot down on the break. As soon as I did, I thought to myself it's too late. It's too close. Suddenly, I hear a voice from inside me saying, "Take your foot off the break." I thought to myself, it's not going to do any good it's too late. I began to argue with the voice, and I pressed down harder. The Lord spoke again, clearer this time, "Take your foot off the break!" I pressed down even harder this time as the blackness seemed to get wider. I pressed so hard on the break that I could feel my heel hitting the front of the car floor. In an instant, I begin to hear the crushing of metal against metal. In slow motion I felt the car moving around in a circle. I heard what sounded like faint cries emerging from the backseat of my car. My children. As we spun, the car seemed to be spinning in slow motion. I looked back to see my girls. I tell them in a slow calm voice, "Everything is going to be okay. We are all going to be okay." The car finally stopped spinning but the cries from the back seat became

louder and louder. The air that was once crisp, cool, and clear was now thick and filled with smoke. I struggle to breathe.

From a once quiet, secure, peaceful sleeping baby I hear a cry that sent a chill up my spine. From a quietly humming little girl, I hear panic begin to rise. "Help, help mommy I can't breathe!" As I turn to reach her, I realize I can't move. My foot is planted like a brick against the floor of the car. I see her reaching for the door handle, she kept trying to grab it, but she couldn't reach to open it. "Help mommy I can't breathe I can't open the door." I immediately push off my heavy foot and lean back to reach for her door. I can't reach it. I begin to pray. I see her door slowly begin to open. Suddenly fear comes over me as I wonder "Who is opening the door?" There are so many people crowding around now and all I can hear is a lot of yelling. I see a woman as she opens the door the rest of the way. She peeks her head in and tells me she's taking my daughter out of the car. I just stare at her. I'm scared. I have no response to give as I see her unbuckle my daughter. My mind is in a panic, "Where is she going? Who is this woman? Will my daughter be okay." All these thoughts are going through my head as I reach for my youngest daughter who is directly behind me. I try to unbuckle her, but I can't. I glance over at my oldest one more time as I see her exiting the car, her eyes wide in fear as she looks at me. I hear the woman telling me that she's got her and she's going to be okay. I watch the back of my daughter as she leaves the car. I hold back tears as I ask the Lord again, "Where is she going, who is she going with? Lord, please keep her safe." The door almost closes but it slowly opens again. I see her tiny face reemerge. As I look at her face, I see fear in her eyes. She looks at me, then she reaches down and grabs her blanket and her stuffed "titi" bunny. I can hear myself telling her, "Everthing is going to be okay," as she turned away from me for a second time. She's holding on tightly to her blankie as she hugs her bunny tightly. As quickly as she entered the car, she was gone again, into the crowded street. I turn to see my baby sitting very still in her car seat behind me. She seemed safe yet she was not saying a word. I try to talk to her, but she just stared straight ahead. I unclipped her from the car seat and try to grab her. I felt pain shoot up the right side of my hand and foot. I try one more time to push off of my foot, as hard as I could to grab hold. I reached and finally got her unbuckled. I tried to pull her out. I couldn't get to her. I think quickly and I grab for my door. It won't open. I panic. I hear yelling, "It's going to blow! You have to get out!" I try again to open the door but its jammed. As I looked back at my daughter, I heard a crack, and the door was pried open. I see a policeman standing there. I try to get out of the car, moving frantically to grab my baby out of the back seat. As I try to get her out, I scan the crowd for my little girl that left the car already. I spot her. She is standing in front of the woman hugging her stuffed animal and clinging to her blankie. "Thank you, Lord, for taking care of my babies." Relief enters my body.

When the EMT's arrived on the scene, they were trying to talk to my youngest but she was not responding. They thought she may be in shock. The EMT's were able to get my youngest out of the car, and they started to move toward the ambulance. I was standing, not able to move. Every time I tried, I felt a shooting pain on the right side of my body. I called out to my oldest daughter. Another EMT came to me as the woman who had taken my daughter from the car came back over to me as well. I was strapped to a gurney, and we all headed to the ambulance together, however they took my youngest, who was also strapped to a gurney, in another ambulance, separate from me and my oldest daughter. I had to hold myself together as I saw her wheeled away. Panic rises within as I try to hold it all together. We headed to the hospital in separate ambulances.

My husband received the call that we were in an accident. He was told to meet us at the hospital. As he tried to head to the hospital, he was rerouted because of the severity of the accident. He had to find an alternate path to the hospital. He wasn't able to get through the area because of the debris that was left from the accident. When he walked into the hospital, I felt some relief to see him. He was asking me questions and wanted to stay with me, but the only thing I could think of was I needed him to find my baby. They had taken my youngest daughter and I didn't know where she was. I kept asking him to please go and find her. He kept telling me she would be fine, and she was with the doctors, but I persisted. I had to find her. Reluctantly, he left my side and went to look. When he found her, there was a brace around her neck and a cut on her forehead. He was told that she had been in shock and wasn't talking but they thought she would recover. Both girls were checked out and discharged from the hospital that day. Praise God they were both protected and were going to be just fine.

I, on the other hand, would have a road of recovery ahead of me. I was sent home on medication with a broken hand and foot. They were not able to operate at the time due to the extensive swelling. When the swelling subsided, I was finally able to get some x-rays, we found out that my heel was shattered, smashed to pieces. I no longer had one. I would need surgery on both my hand and my foot. My hand broke as the result of the impact when the airbag deployed. They put pins and needles in my hand, and they made a new heel for me out of metal and inserted it into my foot. I later found out by one of the nurses that I "lucked out" because the surgeon that was on duty that day was the best there was. I chuckled to myself, "Luck?" I am humble by the grace and mercy of the Lord. *Hebrews 4:16 (ESV)* *"Let us then with confidence draw near to the throne of grace so that we may receive mercy and find grace to help in time of need."* It was not luck that the best surgeon was scheduled to me in that hospital on that day. It was designed by God before the beginning of time. It was the Lord taking care of me, like He always does. The surgeon was so proud of his work on my heel that he stood in the office and showed my husband the beautiful work he had performed on my heel.

I was laid up for about 9 months. Started out in a wheelchair, went to a walker then finally to crutches. I never truly understood the severity of the situation until my last doctor's appointment. The doctor was giving me an update on what to expect next. He began to talk to us about my walking, I kind of smiled and made light of the situation by saying, "I couldn't wait to run on the beach again." The doctor was quiet and looked at me seriously, then he spoke, "You running is the least of my worries, I'm just concerned about you walking again."

I looked at my husband in shock and we left the office in silence. I hadn't realized the extent of damage. My husband was quiet as he said, "We weren't sure if you would walk again." I started PT soon after and by the grace and mercy of the Lord I am able to walk! My ankle gets stiff sometimes, but it is a miracle that I am able to walk, run, hike and bike. The Lord is good, and His mercies are new every morning! *Lamentations 3:22–23(ESV)* *"The steadfast love of the Lord never ceases, his mercies never come to an end; they are new every morning; great is your faithfulness."*

That was a tough time in my life but not only for me. While I was going through it, I didn't really understand the reality of what was happening, but for the family around me, like my husband, they did. I think he may have slept about 5 hours a night for 9 months. My mother came up every day after work with food and to take care of the kids so my husband could sleep. Friends from church would bring meals and one time they came to clean my house. *Galatians 6:2* *"Carry one another's burdens; in this way you will fulfill the law of Christ."*

Looking back, the Lord told me to take my foot off the break, but I didn't listen. I didn't obey. I was too busy questioning God.

It didn't make sense to me. I could only see what was in front of me, I could only see as the world sees, but God understood. *Psalm 33:13–14* reads, *"From heaven the lord looks down and sees all mankind; from his dwelling place he watches all who live on earth."*

He saw the whole picture. Today, I can walk. I am able to walk, run, bike, and live life on two feet because of the love, grace, and mercy of the Lord. He knew. He knew ahead of time. He knew I was going to question Him. Why do I always do that? He took care of us in the midst of all my questioning. He also knew I would repent, and that I would be heartbroken knowing the Lord loved me and was trying to protect me.

He had the woman placed there to take care of my daughter. He had the officer there to get my youngest out of the car, and He had the best doctor at the right hospital at the right time to do my surgery. The Lord showed me grace and mercy that day. He was there; His hand was upon me and my children.

We need to learn; I need to learn to trust the Lord. I need to learn that even though I can't see the whole picture and I don't understand, I need to recognize His still small voice and I need to obey it. *Isaiah 55:8–9* reads, *"For my thoughts are not your thoughts, neither are your ways my ways, declares the Lord, for as the heavens are higher than the earth, so are my ways higher than your ways and my thoughts than your thoughts."*

Lord, may I look back on this time as an encouragement to what You have done and will continue to do. Show me mercy and grace. Lord, may I learn today to listen to Your voice every day. May I seek and listen to Your voice so intently every day that I will never question you again. Lord, You love me. Everything You say to me is because You love me, because You want what is best for me, because You want to protect me, because You only have what's good for me.

Lord, may I grab hold of the love You have for me. May I rejoice in Your direction. May I rejoice in your still small voice knowing You speak to me out of Your love for me. Lord, may I get to the point that when You speak, I hear your voice, I listen, and I trust it. When I fail, because I will, may I repent quickly, receiving your grace and mercy again and again and again. You never tire. In Jesus's name, amen. *Hebrews 4:16* says, *"Let us then approach the throne of grace with confidence, so that we may receive mercy and find grace to help us in our time of need."*

> *The Lord said, "Go out and stand on the mountain in the presence of the Lord, for the Lord is about to pass by." Then a great and powerful wind tore into the mountains apart and shattered the rock before the Lord, but the Lord was not in the wind. After the wind there was an earthquake, but the Lord was not in the earthquake. After the earthquake came a fire, but the Lord was not in the fire. And after the fire came a gentle whisper. When Elijah heard it, he pulled his cloak over his face and went out and stood at the mouth of the cave. So, it was when Elijah heard it, that he wrapped his face in its mantel and went out and stood in the entrance of the cave. Then a voice said to him, "What are you doing here Elijah." (1 Kings 19:11–13)*

It is in the still small voice, the whisper of the Lord, that we hear Him, that we find Him.

Don't turn your back. He is speaking. He loves you.

Proverbs 16:9 ESV

*The heart of a man plans his way, but
the Lord establishes his steps.*

When I became a Christian, the most important thing to me was getting to know Jesus and growing in Him. His love for me was felt so deeply that I wanted, I needed to be able to share it with someone I loved. It's so important to have someone you are spiritually connected with and that you can grow with.

When you get married, you become one. I wanted to be one in all aspects of my life, including spiritually. I needed to be able to share the biggest part of my life, my faith—Jesus, who is the center of my life. Nothing and no one compares to Him. No one could ever love me like Jesus. No one knows what's best for me like Jesus does. Putting my trust in Him was the only thing that mattered.

His way is the best way. Why? Because He is the one who created me. He created you. He knows everything about us, and He created each of us with a purpose. He has this beautiful plan for our life. *Jeremiah 29:11* reads, *"'For I know the plans I have for you,' says the Lord. 'They are plans for good, and not for disaster, to give you a future and a hope.'"*

When the Lord brought me to that person and we talked about having children, the number one thing for me was that they, my children, would grow to know the Lord. All the decisions we made as a couple were so we could raise our children to know the Lord. Having my children in a Christian school was one of those important decisions I wanted to make. When we started to look for houses, we looked for one that was near a Christian school, but it also had to be one that we could afford.

When my first daughter was born, I prayed. All the plans I made were to make sure she would be able to go to a private school. As the time to enroll my oldest in school became closer, I had already had my second daughter. I prayed and prayed to the Lord to make a way. The more I discussed it with my husband, it seemed the Christian school was just too out of our reach.

All the decisions we had made to this point were with this plan in mind. My husband reminded me of the accident I had gotten into just a few years before. He reminded me that would be the same road I would be traveling two times a day, every day, to take the girls to school. He was concerned, and I was completely discouraged.

I cried out to the Lord. I called the school multiple times to try and figure it all out. Did I just not have enough faith? As I sought out people to talk about all that was running through my mind, they all seemed to tell me the same thing—I just needed to have faith. God would work it out. One mentor of mine told me of another family that sent their children to the Catholic school, and they were very happy there.

I continued praying to the Lord, crying out to Him. This may not seem like a big deal to many; however, it was to me. I knew I needed help raising my children. I felt I couldn't do it alone. I knew that not only did my children need a support system, but so did I. I began seeking the Lord for this very thing. As I prayed, the Lord reminded me of the many Catholic schools that were in the town we were actually living in.

This, however, was not what I had planned. As I continued to pray over and over again for the next year, the Lord began to open my heart and eyes to His will for his daughter, not mine. One morning during my devotional time, the Lord began to show me a picture. As I prayed, in my mind's eye, I could see myself standing at a kitchen window. As I gazed out the window, I was looking down on this beautiful long winding driveway. The trees were green. I could see the leaves on the trees blowing gently in the wind.

The driveway was like a beautiful black path that led away from the house. As I looked through the window, I caught a glimpse of the back of my little girl. She was walking down this long, peaceful beautiful driveway. Next to her, I saw Jesus. He was walking next to her. I could see her head turned, looking up at Him. I watched as they walked, hand in hand, down that long pathway together.

I heard the Lord speak to me, "This is the beginning of her walk with me." *Proverbs 16:9* says, *"In their hearts humans plan their course. But the Lord established their steps."* Tears filled my eyes, and I began to weep. As tears rolled down my face, peace began to fill my heart. This is the Lord. This is her Father. This was the beginning of her walk with Him. I needed to let go. As my soul became quiet in the presence of the Spirit, I whispered, "Lord, I trust you."

Over the next few days as I spent time with the Lord, He spoke to me again, *"There comes a time when you will no longer have to tell them about me, they will know."* *Hebrews 8:11* says, *"No longer will they need to teach their neighbor, or say to one another, 'Know the Lord,' because they will all know me, from the least of them to the greatest."* That is our ultimate goal as parents—for our children to know and be known by the Father, for their number one relationship to be with Jesus.

We are not always going to be there, but He will. I will not always get it right. I will not always know the answers, but I know the One who does. It was time for her to grow. It was time for her to begin her journey with Him. To seek Him, not me. We as parents will always be there to guide, protect, and love; but little by little, we need to allow less of us and more of Him.

It was time for a transition to be made from seeking us to seeking Him. We signed her up at the Catholic preschool down the street. I remember getting to walk her to school in the morning. It was a peaceful time. As I walked home, I would find myself praying for her, for my family, and for the town. It was time to hand the baton off. *"Trust the Lord with all your heart and lean not on your own understanding in all your ways, acknowledge him and he will make your path straight"* (Prov. 3:5 ESV).

2 Corinthians 3:16–18

But whenever anyone turned to the Lord, the veil is taken away. Now the Lord is the Spirit, and where the Spirit of the Lord is, there is freedom, and we all, who with unveiled faces contemplate the Lord's glory, are being transformed into His image with every increasing glory which comes from the Lord, who is the Spirit.

As we continued to work on the house and as things began to come together, the Lord began another work in me. The Lord sometimes uses people as a reflection of who we are and how we see ourselves. It may even affect how others see themselves. This was a heartbreaking, eye-opening realization for me.

My oldest daughter was about seven years old when I saw her looking at me through the doorway that was between the kitchen and living room. As I sat in the kitchen, I could see her come out of her room. She kind of stopped as she got halfway through the living room, then she stood there. A little uncomfortable, she looked up at me and said, "Mom, I feel something. I don't know…it seems like… I don't know."

I looked at her through the doorway and asked, "Are you okay?"

"I don't know." Then she said, "I just feel like I'm not pretty. I don't know why. I just don't feel pretty." She stopped and then continued, "I kind of feel ugly." Shocked, I looked up at her. What did I just hear her say? As a mom, hearing these words out of my little girl's mouth cut deep to my soul. As I type, tears well up within me. My baby, my beautiful baby. How? How could she say that? How could she see herself like that?

I stopped and looked up at her from across the room. This beautiful innocent little girl was just standing there looking at me with those beautiful brown eyes. How could she not see how beautiful she was? How could she not know her worth? I looked up at her all these thoughts going through my mind.

I was caught off guard, and I didn't know what to say. When I got my bearings, I asked her, "Why would you say that? Why would you think that?" She stood there and shrugged her shoulders. I looked at her and began to tell her how beautiful she was inside and out. She just looked at me, then walked back into her room. I sat there, my heart heavy. Her comments weighed on me. They stayed with me throughout the day.

The next morning during my devotional time, I found myself thinking about the previous day and what my daughter had said. I began to talk to the Lord about it. My talking turned to prayer, which produced tears. I cried out to the Lord for my daughter. Where do those thoughts come from? How could she see herself in that light? Or should I say in that darkness. My heart broke as I saw my beautiful daughter as God saw her. As I sat, emotionally tired, the Lord spoke. His words cut through to my innermost being. "Now you know how I feel. She sees herself as you see yourself." As the Lord spoke those words, stillness filled the air.

There was no mistaking we were mother and daughter. People called her my twin. I saw my daughter as beautiful. The problem was, I never saw myself as beautiful. I saw myself as ugly on the inside and outside. I always did. I carried that ugliness around with me my entire life. We don't understand the impact the image we have of ourselves will impact our children. I saw myself as ugly, and that grieved the Lord just like my daughter seeing herself that way grieved me.

I was broken. Tears flowed as I repented in prayer. I prayed for her, and I prayed for myself, asking for forgiveness. I continued to lift us both up in prayer. "Lord, give me eyes to see." I began praying for my eyes to be open, as well as my daughter's. I began praying that we would see ourselves as the Lord sees us. Then I thought, *How would I be able to help my daughter be confident in who God created her to be when I myself couldn't see it within me?* I felt the Lord move toward me. He wanted to heal me. He wanted me to be whole.

Gently and quietly, I heard His voice. "Go look in the mirror."

"The mirror?" I asked. I thought about the mirror upstairs.

The Lord spoke again, "I want you to look in the mirror and see what I see." I slowly got up and headed upstairs to the bathroom. As I stood staring at myself in the mirror, the most beautiful thing began to happen. As I looked, I saw what seemed to be scales falling from my eyes. As I looked more intently at myself in the mirror, I began to see right past my eyes, right past those scales that had fallen, and saw straight into my soul through to His Spirit, the Holy Spirit that lives in me. Joy filled my heart. For the first time in my life, I no longer saw myself but Christ in me, and He was beautiful. Tears again began to well up. I was beautiful. I am beautiful because He is beautiful, and He lives in me.

> *Then Ananias went to the house and entered it. Placing his hands-on Saul, he said, "Brother Saul, the Lord-Jesus, who appeared to you on the road as you were coming here—has sent me so that you may see again and be filled with the Holy Spirit." Immediately, something like scales fell from Saul's eyes, and he could see again."* (Acts 9:17–18)

My eyes were opened. The scales were gone, and I could now clearly see the reflection of my Father in me. The Lord is in the business of healing. Beauty is from within, and He is beautiful. We were created in the image of God, and we are beautiful.

Image means "to mirror or reflect." What do you see when you look in the mirror? Whose reflection do you see? When I looked in the mirror, I didn't see the reflection of God. All I saw looking back at me were all my ugly imperfections, all my failures. God changed that. He changed that when He asked Jesus to go to the cross on my behalf. On our behalf. God now sees us through the blood of Christ, the blood that was shed to cover our sins.

I pray for my children as well as for all of you. I'm asking the Lord to take the scales from your eyes that you may see yourself as God sees you—beautiful.

We need to listen to that still small voice of the Lord. It brings healing, restoration, freedom, and joy. *First Peter 3:3–4* says, *"Your beauty should not come from outward adornment, such as elaborate hairstyles and the wearing of gold jewelry or fine clothes. Rather, it should be that of your inner self, the unfading beauty of a gentle and quiet spirit, which is of great worth in God's sight."*

There's a song the Lord used to speak to me. It's by an unknown author, and it's called "Beautiful." In it, the author shares how there was a time that she could see no good in herself. Don't we all feel like that sometimes? But she also sensed that the Lord had planted something, a seed, deep within her and that He would set it free and bring it forth at the appointed time. That is Who our Jesus is.

> *The kingdom of heaven is like a merchant looking for fine pearls. When He found one of great value, He went away and sold everything he had and bought it. (Matt. 13:45)*

You are that pearl of great value. While praying for my youngest daughter recently, the Lord showed me an image. He showed me that deep within her, there was a seed that was planted. I saw the seed begin to flourish, and a flower begin to grow. As it began to grow, something came—whether word or deed—and cut it down. I could see that with some nurturing, that seed would again take root and spring forth.

That seed is planted in each one of us. As life comes, we sometimes allow the world, the enemy, to cut down and take away all that the Lord has begun to do in us. I pray that little seed that the Lord has planted in all of us will continue to be called forth to completion. I pray that the seed planted will be allowed to continue to bloom and flourish to fruition so that we can become all that God has called us to be.

A LIFE WORTH SAVING

The righteous will flourish like a palm tree, they will grow like a cedar of Lebanon; planted in the house of the Lord, they will flourish in the courts of our God. (Psalms 92:12–13)

John 17:14–16

I have given them your word and the world has hated them, for they are not of the world any more than I am of the world. My prayer is not that you take them out of the world but that you protect them from the evil one. They are not of the world, even as I am not of it. Sanctify them by the truth, your word is truth, as you sent me into the world, I have sent them into the world. For them I sanctify myself, that they too may be truly sanctified.

After my accident, the thought of driving the children to the Christian school didn't sit well with my husband. He felt like it was a lot of driving, and he wanted us all to be safe. By this time, we were graced with another blessing, another daughter named Olivia. Not only did he see the drive as too much for me to take every day, but financially, he felt like it was a big risk.

I was doing well financially with my cleaning jobs; however, all my jobs were in the opposite direction from the Christian school. We had two children in the Catholic school, one full time and one part time, and we were looking at our third child entering school in a few years. I prayed and I prayed.

We began looking for houses again. We again started looking for housing close to the Christian school. There was none we could find. In frustration and disappointment, I started to look at houses in other towns where there were better school systems. In a few years, we were looking at three children in school; we needed to make a decision.

A LIFE WORTH SAVING

One morning during my prayer time, the Lord spoke to my heart, "In the world, not of this world." *Lord, what does that mean?* I asked. *First John 17:14–16* says, *"I have given them your word and the world has hated them, for they are not of the world any more than I am of the world. My prayer is not that you take them out of the world but that you protect them from the evil one. They are not of the world, even as I am not of it. Sanctify them by the truth, your word is truth, as you sent me into the world, I have sent them into the world. For them I sanctify myself, that they too may be truly sanctified."*

The Lord spoke to me through His word, and I heard him. "My prayer is not that you take them out of the world but that you protect them from the evil one." I listened. We found a house the next town over, and we moved. I remember calling a friend of mine to tell her we were moving. "You're moving in the wrong direction!" I felt a deep sadness. I wanted to be surrounded by my people, my friends.

The Lord was faithful to my children. It was the first year in the new school, and my daughter's teacher was a Christian. The Lord never left them. When my two oldest girls were in high school, they both had Christian coaches—one in volleyball, the other in cross-country and track. God is faithful. When my youngest went to school, her aide was a Christian. God surrounded my children through the public school with great Christian mentors.

At the same time all this was going on, our longtime pastor was called to a different state. So many changes. With the new pastor, some people started to leave the church. Then a few years later, we had another pastor change. More and more people started leaving and finding other churches. Our church, our support system, was becoming fractured. Most of our friends lived in the area of the Christian school; some still were able to maintain connections. It was more difficult for us. Not only did we move to a different town, but now, we also had to find a different church. It was getting exceedingly more and more difficult for me.

When I first became saved, the Lord lavished me with His love, His healing. I was taken in and mentored by so many wonderful, godly people. I met my husband. He got saved. We were married. We served at church—my husband on the worship team, I in women's ministry. The Lord used us, and we grew. Now I felt lost and alone. I felt like that person in scripture that was being blown by the wind or the seed that fell on the wrong soil.

> *But when you ask, you must believe and not doubt, because the one who doubts is like a wave of the sea, blown and tossed by the wind. (James 1:6)*

> *As he was scattering the seed, some fell along the path, and the birds came and ate it up. Some fell on rocky places where it didn't have much soil. It sprang up quickly because the soil was shallow. But when the sun came up the plants were scorched, and they withered because they had no root. Other seed fell among thorns, which grew up and choked the plants. Still other seed fell on good soil where it produced a crop. Whoever has ears let them hear. (Matt. 13:4–9)*

Did I not have faith? Did I doubt? Did we make a mistake? The Lord reminded me, "Be in the world but not of the world." I had to trust Him.

John 4:6

Jacobs well was there, and Jesus, tired as he was from the journey, sat down by the well. It was about noon.

Having three children, moving to a new town and a new house, seeking for and changing churches—it was all too much. My husband worked two jobs and was going to school to be a teacher. It was a lot. I tried to read the Bible and spend time in prayer every day, like I always had, but it was getting harder and harder. There was always an interruption. I even tried to get up earlier, but no matter what I did, I just couldn't get the time alone with the Lord I needed. Either the kids would wake up or the dog would need to go out, something would always come up.

No matter what time I got up, my time with the Lord was always interrupted. I was sad. I was lonely. I cried out to the Lord in anguish, and he answered. But the answer was a tough one. Through my tears, I heard Him say, "You will set the tone for this house."

I broke down. "Lord, that's too much. I can't take on all that responsibility. It's too much for me to carry." *Matthew 11:28* says, *"Come to me, all you who are weary and burdened, and I will give you rest."* I turned my back and gave up.

That day, I made a decision—a decision to turn away. The Lord was telling me that I would set the tone for the family, and I just couldn't hold it together anymore. I love the Lord, but I began to shut down. I had gotten to that place, to the place I never thought I could ever or would ever get to. When I was first saved, I remember seeing people during worship that were not outwardly worshipping, not raising their hands, not kneeling; and I would say to the Lord, "Lord, how can they not fully worship you? How can they not worship you outwardly, in spirit and in truth?"

I thought to myself, *I will never get to that place, I will always worship you*. Well, I was here. Broken. *John 4:6 (AMP)* says, *"Jacob's well was there. So Jesus, tired as he was from His journey, sat down by the well, it was about the sixth hour."* Jesus got tired. I was tired. I felt like I needed someone to come hold up my arms like Aaron and Hur did for Moses, but there was no one. *Exodus 17:12–14* reads, *"When Moses' hands grew tired, they took a stone, and put it under him and he sat on it. Aaron and Hur held his hands up—one on one side, one on the other—so that his hands remained steady until sunset. So Joshua overcame the Amalekite army with the sword."*

The words were ringing in my ear, "Please, Lord, don't ever let me get to that point in my Christian walk." Well, I was there. Somehow, it crept up on me. I tried to talk to my husband, but he was so busy with work and school. He was doing his best. I knew he was, but I needed him. I needed someone. I was overwhelmed. He was frustrated. I remember saying to him at one point, "Don't you dare leave me now!" I knew he wouldn't. That's something the Lord had settled years ago before we were even married.

Those chains had been broken, and this generation had been set free. But this was a tough time, and we were going through it. We had been married about ten years, and honestly, there were times during this period in our lives that I wondered why I ever married this man. I am sure those thoughts crossed his mind as well, but we had made a commitment to each other. The Lord had broken the generational curse of divorce. I knew it. We never even spoke of it.

I knew we would be okay, but I won't lie, it was hard. I remember one night at about ten thirty, my youngest was wheezing so badly, I had to take her to the hospital. I called the ambulance and called my husband. He worked an hour away, and he was already almost there. He couldn't come back. I had no one. I had to make a quick decision. We couldn't all go in the ambulance, so I sent my oldest in the ambulance with my youngest, and I followed behind in the car with my middle child. The officer asked if there was anyone I could call: a neighbor, a family member, anyone? There was no one.

I was alone and broken. It was the beginning of a downward spiral. I was angry, I was stressed, and I was emotionally drained. Without family, without an established church, I found myself in a dark place. Looking back, I wish I had trusted the Lord more.

The anxiety consumed me, and then the panic attacks started. I remember my first panic attack. It happened when I was forty. I was driving home from the gym one Saturday morning, and I had to pull over and call my husband. My heart was racing. I was having trouble seeing, and I couldn't breathe. It was so bad that I turned around and drove into the fire station because I didn't think I would make it home. I thought I was having a heart attack. Satan really began to have his way with me.

My fear and anxiety had gotten so bad that I would wake up in the middle of the night and just pace the floor. Some nights, I would find myself in the entryway lying on the bench just so I could breathe. I needed fresh air. Sometimes, I would quietly climb into my oldest daughter's room and curl up next to her in bed. I didn't want to be alone.

One morning, the kids came downstairs to wait for the bus, and I was so full of anxiety that I asked my middle daughter to sit with me just for a minute. I held her hand. I needed to. My husband worked third shift at the time. I called the ambulance two more times that year until I finally understood that it was not my heart at all. My father died of a heart attack in his fifties, and my doctor put me on fish oil when I turned forty. She told me she wanted to be proactive. I think that struck me; and that's when, looking back, I realized the fear of dying crept in.

We need the Lord. We all need the Lord. There is freedom in knowing and recognizing that in this life, we need each other and we need the Lord. *Galatians 5:1* reads, *"It is for freedom that Christ has set us free. Stand firm, then and do not let yourselves be burdened again by a yoke of slavery."*

During this time, the Lord showed me a picture of my husband and I. We were little children. I could see us both, maybe seven or eight years of age. We were running down this beautiful hill full of tall grass and dandelions. We both had big smiles on our faces, then suddenly, we both began to stumble and fall. We were getting tangled in the tall grass.

In the vision, I saw the Lord gently reach down His hand from heaven, scoop us up, and hold us in His arms. He picked us both back up and placed us back on our feet. Our Father sees us as little children. We are His children, and these two of His children were stumbling. Yet He was there. He hadn't let us go. *Psalm 40:2* says, *"He lifted me out of the slimy pit out of the mud and mire. He set my feet on a rock and gave me a firm place to stand."*

Psalms 78:6–7

So, the next generation would know them—even the children yet to be born—and they in turn would tell their children. Then they would put their trust in God and would not forget His deeds but would keep His commands.

With the new move and the changes in our church of seventeen years, we began to pray and seek the Lord for a new church. We began praying and visited a few in the area. We were looking for an established church that shared the gospel and had a strong youth group that the girls could grow in. We couldn't find one with the fullness of our old church. Our search led us to a church that was right over the state line about fifteen minutes away. Our kids joined the children's programs, and in time, we made this our new home. My husband joined the worship team, and I the women's ministry.

We all began to grow again and make some friends. All three of our children made the decision to be baptized. One of my daughters started a Bible study in her school with a friend from youth group. They were beginning to step out in faith. My daughter came home after one of the first Bible study meetings and told me that a boy from school came to the study. They prayed for him, and he received the Lord.

She went on to tell me the most amazing part of the story, His story. The boy was heading to the counselor's office to tell the counselor that he wanted to end his life. While walking to the office, he saw the Bible study sign that the girls had made and posted on the wall. He decided instead to go to the study. During that very first Bible study, the girls shared the gospel of Christ with him.

This child of God who intended to end his life heard about the good news of Christ. He heard about how he had a Father in heaven that created him, loved him, and died for him. The Lord is in the business of finding the one. *Matthew 18:12* says, *"If a man owns a hundred sheep, and one of them wanders away, will he not leave the ninety-nine on the hills and go to look for the one that wandered off?"* The Bible study didn't last very long, but it was there at the right time to reach a boy that was lost but now had been found.

How about the time my daughter invited her friend to youth group? Week after week, we would pick her up and take her with us. She became part of our family. She came to know Jesus and gave her life to Christ. What about when that friend turned around and FaceTimed another and talked to her about Jesus and that friend recommitted her life to Christ?

Why was my life worth saving? One life saved reaches another life and another and another. How about me, being a stalker mom, checking my children's social media accounts? I saw a post from my daughter. It was just a picture of her, but what struck me was what was written under her post. Among all the you're-beautiful comments, I saw one that stuck out from the rest: "TBH [to be honest] you are gorgeous, and you have a great heart for God."

This momma's heart is blessed. How about when your high school daughter volunteers at an after-school program for kids in the special Olympics just to hang out and spend time loving on them. What about when your daughter goes to a youth conference/retreat and, during worship, does all she can to stand yet ultimately falls to her knees in the overwhelming presence of Almighty God?

These are the beautiful moments a mother will forever treasure in her heart. To the daughter who was led to go on a mission's trip to Haiti. Knowing no one, she stepped out in faith and went anyway. She took the time to go to meeting after meeting to prepare for her trip, learning the language and the culture. She did it because she knew God called her to go. One of her favorite parts of the mission's trip was spending time in the word every morning and every night with the leader and her group. She was growing every day.

The joy-filled pictures of her and her mission mates loving on those orphans will forever impact them and her, and again is a blessing to this momma's heart. Another mission trip to be planned would be thwarted by the untimely death of a friend. Those plans never came to pass, but the hope of a reunion in heaven brings solace and peace. How about the time I was co-leading a Bible study on the power of the praying parent and my middle daughter came home with a foot injury (she's a runner). Then my oldest came home from youth service talking about prayer and the power of the laying on of hands during prayer. The three of us came together and prayed for my daughter's healing. She woke up the next morning, and the pain was gone.

This is when you take a step back and realize that you are not perfect, but He is perfect. You realize you cannot always be there, but He can. He has our children in the palm of His hands. He is in your children's life; He is guiding them. Let's take a step back and look and see what the Lord is doing in our children's lives, and let's continue to pray that they have eyes to see and ears to hear what the Spirit of the Lord is saying to them. Let's continue to lift up our loved ones to Him in prayer and watch Him do His mighty work in their lives.

Lord, why did you save me? *Psalm 78:4* reads, *"We will not hide them from their children; but tell to the coming generation the glorious deeds of the Lord, and his might and the wonders that he has done."*

Joel 2:25–26 (ESV)

I will restore to you the years that the swarming locusts has eaten, the hopper, the destroyer, and the cutter, my great army, which I sent among you. You shall eat in plenty and be satisfied, and praise the name of the Lord your God, who has dealt wondrously with you. And my people shall never again be put to shame.

Mother's Day was coming up, and the church we attended was having a Mother's Day brunch. I was part of the women's ministry team, and I was asked to speak. I accepted and began to pray. While I was praying and preparing for the Mother's Day prayer breakfast, I began to get overwhelmed with my own insecurity and imperfections as a mom.

Although I knew the Lord called me to speak, I couldn't help but think of the many other women better equipped to speak on mothers than me. One day, as I was grappling with these feelings of insecurity, I went to the mailbox. As I retrieved the mail, I realized the Lord sent me a beautiful nugget through a Christian ministry magazine. It was an answer to my prayer.

As I took the little magazine out of the mailbox, I sat down and began to read it. The Lord began to speak directly to my heart. He knew what I needed. He knew what all of us women needed to hear. What He spoke to me was, there are no perfect moms. It's an impossible standard. We are all going to miss the mark sometimes. But what we do have is hope in a perfect God who is always ready and willing to extend to us His perfect grace, love, and mercy every time we seek it.

Just breathe that in for a minute. Can we all just let that minister to our souls for a minute? This was the confirmation and direction I needed from the Lord. It was a reminder that, yes, I am not perfect; yet you, Lord, would again use me in my areas of weakness. You called me anyway, and you had placed something specific on my heart to share. I smiled to myself at the faithfulness of the Lord. I breathed in a sigh of relief, thanking the Lord again for the reminder that He doesn't expect perfection, just faithfulness.

> *And we know that in all things God works for the good of those who love Him, who have been called according to His purpose. (Rom. 8:28)*

God is not looking for perfect moms. That we will never be. He is looking for moms who are willing to humble themselves before Him and seek His face. God knows about our imperfections, our children know all about our imperfections, and our husbands know as well. How about we humbly embrace our imperfection, hoping and knowing that by accepting them, we can acknowledge them and allow the Lord to change us day by day in hopes of showing how the Lord's way is perfect not ours. *Psalm 25:9 (ESV)* says, *"He guides the humble in what is right and teaches them His way."*

The Lord brought me back to the book of Samuel. In 1 Samuel, we met Hannah. Hannah is a perfect example of a godly mom. She was troubled, yet she is humble and sought the Lord. *Romans 12:12* reminds me of Hannah as well: *"Be joyful in hope patient in affliction faithful in prayer."*

As I continued to pray, I began to read *1 Samuel 1:10*. *"In her deep anguish Hannah prayed to the Lord, weeping bitterly. And she made a vow saying, 'Lord Almighty, if you will only look on your servant's misery and remember me, and not forget your servant but give her a son, than I will give him to the Lord for all the days of his life, and no razor will ever be used on his head.'"*

As a mom, Hannah got it right. In her anguish, she humbled herself before the Lord. In *1 Samuel 1:13–15*, it goes on to say, *"Hannah was praying in her heart and her lips were moving but her voice was not heard. Eli thought she was drunk. 'Not so, my lord,' Hannah replied, 'I am a woman who is deeply troubled. I was pouring out my soul to the Lord.'"*

Have you ever prayed for your children like this? I have. This reminds me of a few times in my life I have prayed for my children: when I prayed for my oldest daughter's dedication, when I prayed for the school, when I prayed for their salvation and countless other times. Have you ever poured out your heart to the Lord for your children like Hannah did?

There was another time I remember calling out to the Lord like this. It was a time in my life that I was struggling to understand one of my children. I was praying to the Lord because I no longer knew what to do. As I cried out to the Lord for my daughter, the Lord kept bringing to my mind "love." As I continued to hear the word *love*, a heavy realization came to me. Right in the middle of our entryway, I fell to my knees. With tears in my eyes, I confessed to the Lord what He already knew, "Lord, I don't know how to love! Lord, show me!" He brought me to 1 *Corinthians 13:4–7*. *"Love is patient, love is kind. It does not envy. It does not boast. It is not proud. It does not dishonor others, it is not self-seeking, it is not easily angered, it keeps no records of wrongs. Love does not delight in evil but rejoices with the truth. It always protects, always trusts, always hopes, always preserves."* The Lord spoke to me about writing this scripture in calligraphy, on the stairs that led upstairs. This scripture spoke to me just as many others did throughout my life's journey. I needed to listen to the Lord, meditate on the scriptures, and write them throughout the house. They became reminders to me, as well as to my family.

As I continued to prepare for the Mother's Day breakfast, I read how Eli answered Hannah in *1 Samuel 1:17: "Go in peace, and may the God of Israel grant you what you have asked of him."* Hannah became pregnant and gave birth to a son. *She named him Samuel "because I asked the Lord for him"* (verse 20). Hannah made a promise to the Lord that if he gave her a son, she would give him back to the Lord. Hannah kept her promise, and when Samuel was weaned, she took him and brought him to the house of the Lord.

First *Samuel 1:26–28* reads, *"Pardon me, my lord, as surely as you live, I am the woman who stood here beside you praying to the Lord. I prayed for this child. The Lord has granted me what I asked of him. So now I give him to the Lord for his whole life he will be given over to the Lord."* Hannah continued her prayers, and they turned into praise. In *1 Samuel 2*, Hannah begins praising and thanking the Lord for all He had done for her. In *1 Samuel 2:21*, it says, *"And the Lord was gracious to Hannah; she gave birth to three sons and two daughters."* The Lord was gracious to Hannah, and he has been to me as well. I have been blessed with three beautiful daughters. Pray and be encouraged. Allow the Lord to remind you of how He has been gracious to you.

I shared earlier how I co-led a Bible study called *Praying Circles around Your Children*. In that book, it references verse 26 of *1 Samuel 2*: *"And the boy Samuel continued to grow in stature and in favor with the Lord and with people."* This has been my prayer, as a mom, for my children. It's a bold prayer to pray. Pray it anyway. Pray that your children will grow in stature and in favor with the Lord and with people. What a powerful prayer to pray over our children. It's a prayer of boldness.

Our children aren't perfect, and they are never going to be. When we see them start to struggle, let's hold on to the promise God gives us as moms in *Proverbs 22:6 (ESV)*, *"Train your children in the way they should go and when they are old, they will not depart from it."* We need to hold on to as many promises from God that we can. We need to trust in Him!

In the first house we bought, the Lord had put on my heart the scripture in *Deuteronomy 11:18–20* that says, *"Fix these words of mine in your hearts and minds. Tie them as symbols on your hands and bind them on your foreheads. Teach them to your children, talk about them when you sit at home and when you walk along the road, when you lie down and when you get up. Write them on the door frames of your house and on your gates, so that your days and the days of your children may be many in the land the Lord swore to give your ancestors."* I wrote this scripture around our built-in.

Back in the book of *1 Samuel 3:2–9*, it says,

> One night Eli whose eyes were becoming so weak that he could barely see, was lying down in his usual place. The lamp of God had not yet gone out and Samuel was laying down in the house of the Lord where

> *the ark of God was. Then the Lord called Samuel. Samuel answered, "Here I am. And he ran to Eli and said, "Here I am; you called me." But Eli said, "I did not call you; go back and lie down." So, he went and laid down. Again, the Lord called "Samuel!" And Samuel got up and went to Eli and said, "Here I am: you called me.". Then Eli realized that the Lord was calling the boy. So Eli told Samuel, "Go and lie down and if he calls you, say, "Speak, Lord, for your servant is listening," So Samuel did.*

There are times the Lord calls us. Be prepared to listen. There is also going to come a time, a day, that the Lord will begin to speak to and call our children. He will begin to speak directly to them just like He did with Samuel. I remember when it happened with my oldest daughter. I didn't recognize it at first, and I struggled with it a bit. I was her mom, and I didn't want to let her go. I still find myself wanting to guide her, which is healthy, but we need to let them go and allow them to seek the Lord for themselves.

We need to encourage them to listen and obey. I was struggling with this a little and still do sometimes, but the Lord gave me this scripture to encourage me.

> *This is the covenant I will establish with the people of Israel after that time, declares the Lord. I will put my laws in their minds and write them on their hearts. I will be their God, and they will be my people. No longer will they teach their neighbor or say to one another know the Lord, because they will all know me. From the least of them to the greatest. For I forgive their wickedness and will remember their sins no more." (Heb. 8:10–12)*

The Lord has put His laws in our hearts as well as the hearts and minds of our children. He is their God, not only ours. They are His children. There will come a point that we no longer need to tell them about God because they will already know Him. That doesn't mean we stop being their parents. Hannah still made Samuel a robe every year and took it to him. He was her son. It just means less of us and more of the Lord, which is exactly what our goal as a mom should be.

We don't need to stand in the gap; Jesus is standing in the gap! As I allowed the Lord to speak directly to them, I began to see the work of His hand in their lives. One of my daughter's friends was an atheist. He told her he hated Christians, but he liked her because even though they disagreed on a lot of issues, he could see a love of Christ in her that he doesn't usually see in Christians. I continue to lift them up in prayer and guide them, but they are ultimately the Lord's. I pray they seek Him and listen and obey.

Am I a perfect mom? As you can see through my writings, I am not. I will never be. These stories are all about my weaknesses as a person, as a mom, as a wife and as a Christian.

I am reminded that there will never be a perfect mom. Least of all me. We just do not exist. However, we do have a perfect God Who is always there extending grace, mercy, and love to each of us. As we go through this journey of motherhood, He will use all of our shortcomings and all of our insecurities, to bring our children unto Himself. Where we fall short, we can trust that the Lord will come and fill in those gaps perfectly.

What about our moms? This applies to them as well. I have shared my struggles with my own mother. I have shared how there was a time in my life that my relationship with my mom was less than perfect. I would literally get sick to my stomach heading to her house. When I sought the Lord, He brought me to scripture, and healing took place in me.

You can't expect people to understand; and you can't make people apologize for behaviors. We have to understand that they too are human, and they too are imperfect. They make mistakes as well. When we allow the Lord to heal us, we can forgive our parents. We can accept them for who they are and where they have come from. In that, we can finally receive our healing. No mother is perfect, but no matter how wide the gulf may be between you and your mother,

God can bridge that gap. *Ephesians 4:32* says, *"Be kind and compassionate to one another forgiving each other, just as Christ forgave you."*

Recently my family had gone away on vacation. I, unfortunately, had to stay behind for work. I had a medical issue that I thought I was handling, but on the second day of their trip, I was not. Panicked, I picked up the phone and called my mother. Through my tears, I asked her to come stay with me. She didn't hesitate. She packed up her things for the night and came right over. I felt peace and comfort knowing I wouldn't be alone. The next day I went to work, and she went home, only to return for the next three nights to stay with me.

After she left, I sat, reflecting on the sacrifice she made. The Lord began to soften my heart. I realized that the sacrifice she made was for no one else, only me. My heart was overwhelmed with gratitude. In the past, my mother had been there for my family, but this time, it felt different. This time when I called, she came just to be with me. I truly understood the love my mother had for me, the love she had for me all along. I was finally able to fully receive and embrace that love.

On one of the last mornings, she woke up and shared her daily devotional with me. She knew I had been feeling anxious, and she felt led to share the message of hope and trust she had just read about the Lord. It was a beautiful full-circle moment.

I can't help but think of the song by Kari Jobe, "The Blessing." In it, she sings of the Lord's favor being passed down from generation to generation of those who loved Him. I had always thought about the generation starting with me, but on that day, the Lord revealed to me that at that moment, my mother was part of that journey.

"The Lord will guide you always; He will satisfy your needs in a sun-scorched land. And will strengthen you frame. You will be like a well-watered garden, like a spring whose water never fails" (Isaiah 58:11).

Where is God leading you?

To humility? *Psalm 25:9* says, *"He guides the humble in what is right and teaches them his way."*

To forgive? *Ephesians 4:32* says, *"Be kind and compassionate to one another forgiving each other, just as Christ forgave you."*

Is He wanting to heal you? *Psalm 147:3* says, *"He heals the broken hearted and binds up their wounds."*

Is He calling you to put your trust in Him? *Proverbs 3:5–6* says, *"Trust in the Lord with all your heart and lean not on your own understanding in all your ways submit to him and he will make your* path *straight."*

Do you need to admit and accept that you are not perfect? *Psalm 19:7* says, *"The law of the Lord is perfect, refreshing the soul. The statues of the Lord are trustworthy, making wise the simple."*

Let's trust the Lord with our faults, with our imperfections. Let's put our trust in Him.

The Lord has done so much healing in my life. I have been able to forgive my mom, to forgive my family. They love us just like we love our own children. They did the best they could, just like we are trying to do with our children. We have all tried to do what is best for our children. We do it with love always at the center.

The Lord has given me this understanding, it is a blessing to let go. It is a blessing to receive love and compassion from the Lord and be able to extend it to others. I praise and thank the Lord for the healing and restoration He has done in my relationship with my mother. I'm so thankful to have the relationship I have with her today. She is a blessing. *Joel 2:25–26 (ESV)* reads, *"I will restore to you the years that the swarming locust has eaten, the hopper, the destroyer, and the cutter, my great army, which I sent among you. You shall eat in plenty and be satisfied, and praise the name of the lord your God, who has dealt wondrously with you. And my people shall never again be put to shame."*

Matthew 6:2

So, when you give to the needy, do not announce it with trumpet, as the hypocrites do in the synagogues and on the streets, to be honored by others. Truly I tell you, they have received their reward in full.

We were all involved and growing at our new church, but as time went on, my anxiety grew. As I struggled, I noticed the biggest part that was missing for me in this church. It was prayer. We came from a church of prayers. Everyone prayed all the time. It didn't matter what it was or who it was; we would all come together in prayer.

We prayed before worship, before service, during the service, and at the end of service. We also had teams available if you needed prayer after service. That's what we did; we prayed. Prayer for me is like breathing. Out of normal conversations, prayer emerges. *Philippians 4:6–7* says, *"Do not be anxious about anything, but in every situation, by prayer and petition, with thanksgiving, present your requests to God. And the peace of God which transcends all understanding, will guard your hearts and your minds in Christ Jesus."*

In this church, it was different. As I watched, I began to notice that if someone was hurting or struggling, prayer wasn't utilized. Instead, there were suggestions—a suggestion to see a different kind of doctor or maybe try an herbal remedy. Those are all good suggestions, but there was no prayer. I remember reaching out at one point to someone who had been in the church for a long time, and I asked for prayer. She gave me a questionable look then looked around and said, "Oh, I think that should be okay. I think people pray for each other." The response took me off guard. It was then I realized prayer was not the breath of this church.

Prayer was my lifeline, and as I noticed the deficiency in that area, I pulled back on my prayer not because I wanted to but because it just wasn't done. I noticed the name of Jesus wasn't spoken much in prayer. The pastor preached the word, and the Bible studies were biblical. It was just missing something; I was missing something. God created me to pray. I needed that communication with Him in community with others.

In this environment, I found myself not seeking the Lord and sort of asking others. It was strange and not who I was, not who God created me to be. But it was so normal here. It was the way it was done in this church, so it just began to happen naturally. As time went on, my anxiety became greater and greater. It was like I couldn't breathe anymore. I began desperately seeking women of faith, women of prayer.

The one thing that was strong in this church was servanthood. Servanthood in and of itself is very biblical; however, during this time in my life, the Lord was speaking something different to me. He was telling me "to be." Just *be*.

All around me was this hustle and bustle of life, and it felt like it had infiltrated the church. As I looked as I prayed, I realized the world had crept its way in. As the church continued to speak "serve," I struggled. The Lord was telling me to *be*. I kept hearing, "If you're not serving, you're not growing." I continued to serve, thinking, *Jesus came to serve, so I must serve too.*

Something inside me was not at rest. Something was wrong. How could the Lord be telling me one thing and the church be telling me another? I am to submit to the leaders in authority; they are placed there by the Lord. *Hebrews 13:17* says, *"Have confidence in your leaders and submit to their authority, because they keep watch over you as those who must give an account. Do this so that their work will be joy, not a burden, for that would be of no benefit to you."*

"So what is going on, Lord?" I started asking the question. "Is it me? Why am I sensing something different?" The Lord spoke to my heart one day through a post I saw on social media about serving. I know it's an unlikely place to have the Lord speak, but it really hit me. "Was the church serving itself?" As I read, it became clearer. "Was the church giving glory to the servers but not glory to the Lord?"

It had become a competition among the members of the church. Who would get the prize at the trunk or treat or who had the ugliest sweater at Christmastime? Who served at the men's breakfast? Who brought the breakfast, whose dish was the best? We seemed to be looking inward and not outward. *Matthew 6:2* says, *"So when you give to the needy, do not announce it with trumpets. As the hypocrites do in the synagogues and on the streets, to be honored by others. Truly I tell you, they have received their reward in full."* I didn't see anyone going beyond the four walls of the church. It seemed everyone wanted their recognition and was in fact receiving their reward in full.

The article I read was about true service—the one that is unseen, not the service that was being shouted from the rooftops. The scripture that came to mind is in *Mark 10:35–45 (ESV)*.

> *And James and John, the sons of Zebedee, came up to him and said to him, "Teacher, we want you to do for us whatever we ask of you." And he said to them, "What do you want me to do for you?" And they said to him, "Grant us to sit, one at your right hand and one at your left, in your glory." Jesus said to them, "You do not know what you are asking. Are you able to drink the cup that I drink, or to be baptized with the baptism with which I am baptized?" And they said to him, "We are able." And Jesus said to them, "The cup that I drink you will drink, and with the baptism with which I am baptized you will be baptized. But to sit at my right hand or at my left is not mine to grant, but it is for those for whom it has been prepared." When the ten heard it, they began to be indignant at James and John. And Jesus called them to him and said to them, "You know that those who are considered rulers of the Gentiles lord it over them, and their great one's exercise authority over*

them. But it shall not be so among you, but whoever would be great among you must be your servant. And whoever would be first among you must be slave to all."

This is human nature. We can get there quickly, can't we? What position could get closer to a pastor or to a leader? Who was that someone to get you recognition? Just like James and John wanted to be "seated" at the right and the left. Serving had become a status to attain, a status to achieve. It was service to be seen.

In *Ephesians 2:8–10 (ESV)*, it says, *"For it is by grace you have been saved, through faith and this is not for yourselves, it is a gift of God—not by works. So that no one can boast. For we are His workmanship. Created in Christ Jesus for good works, which God prepared beforehand that we should walk in them."* Our gifts are to be used to bring glory to God, not glory to ourselves.

Matthew 5:16 reads, *"In the same way, let your light shine before others, that they may see our good deeds and glorify your Father in heaven."* It had become to some the pride of serving and the importance of who was the one being served. The glory wasn't going to God; it was going to each other. The pressure to serve was causing division, anxiety, and boastfulness. It became about what everyone was doing, not what the Lord was doing.

At youth group, the senior high school kids were encouraged to serve and, once serving, were allowed to sign up and be part of the youth team. My oldest served on Sunday mornings in the toddler room. She signed up to be part of the team. Most of the other teens served under the youth pastor or his wife. After she signed up to be a part of the team, the youth pastor stopped me and he told me my daughter couldn't join the team because she wasn't serving. I told him that she had been serving in the toddler room for quite some time. He looked shocked; he didn't know. She had been serving unassumingly.

It seemed like judgment reigned over wisdom and humility. There seemed to be a shift happening in the church and in the leadership that was quite different than when we had first gotten there seven years before, or maybe we just hadn't seen it? It was no longer relational; it had turned to works. Serving wasn't about the calling on your life; it was about who and where you served and who knew about it. It no longer seemed to be as the Lord intended when He called us to serve.

I continued to ponder the word *serve*. I had been truly seeking the Lord because my soul had not been at rest; I had begun to wrestle with the word *serve*, not because I don't believe we are to serve but because of the way the word seemed to be distorted. For some reason, when I heard the word *serve*, I sort of started to cringe. My reaction to the word really began to bother me.

As a Christ follower, I knew serving was biblical, so I began to seek the Lord about what was going on in my heart. What I found was that it wasn't the word itself; it was the connotation that seemed to come with the word *serve*. I continued to seek the Lord. *Lord, what does it truly mean to serve? Jesus served so we serve, but how did Jesus serve? Did He serve Himself? Did He serve for recognition?* He most certainly did receive recognition but the kind that landed Him on the cross to suffer and die for our sins.

Did He serve to receive anything? Praise? Accolades? No. Not Jesus. He served selflessly. I began to think about how He went. He didn't stay within the four walls of a church. Jesus went. He served in humility. He did not serve to be noticed. He did not serve to be thanked. He did not serve to be puffed up. He served in humility, out of love for his children and those that were lost. He served so that people would come to know Christ. He did as the Father said. He served the Father. He served others so that they would be set free. *John 5:19* says, *"Very truly I tell you, the Son can do nothing by himself; he can do only what he sees his Father doing, because whatever the Father does the Son also does."*

I was in women's ministry and serving with the youth two times a week. I know the Lord was calling me to *be*, but I felt the pressure to continue to serve. I continued to pray and seek the Lord. I was invited to a Bible study at one of the women's homes. Most of the people there were family. It felt nice to be included, but deep down inside, I felt something in my spirit. As time went by, our families connected. We were invited to family things, and my circle of friends began to grow. However, as time went by, the truth of the relationship began to reveal itself.

The women's ministry team was expanding. We were asked to seek the Lord and share if He had put anyone on our hearts that we felt led to ask to join. The Lord placed one of the women on my heart. She was humble and kind. She loved the Lord. As I extended an invite, I almost immediately began to feel tension. I received a call asking me if I could write and recommend the other women in her circle.

I knew God specifically put that one woman on my heart. However, I emailed the pastor's wife not just about the one but, as it turned out, two others. I didn't feel at peace, but I added them all to the list and submitted it. The first meeting, I became aware that we were not friends. It had been about serving in women's ministry.

For a year and a half, my husband would tell me, "Hunny, be careful. They are not your friends." Those words came back to my mind during that first meeting. He had warned me; I didn't listen. The need for relationship outweighed the warning.

The Lord used this time to allow me to take a step back from women's ministry as well as youth ministry. I began to submit to the Lord's leading for me to *be*. Romans 8:7 *(ESV)* reads, *"For the mind that is set on the flesh is hostile to God, for it does not submit to God's law; indeed, it cannot."* It was time to humble myself before the Lord and submit to His calling for me to just *be*.

Psalm 4:8

In peace I will lie down and sleep, for you alone, Lord, make me dwell in safety.

Let that sweet truth just settle down deep within your soul. I have heard that it is written 365 times in the Bible: "Do not fear." One for each day of the year. If we can just meditate on His word and allow Him to build us up, oh how sweet that peace will be.

I remember when I first started to struggle with fear and anxiety. Actually, there were two things that attributed to it. One was after I had my third child. I believe I had postpartum depression. I remember going to the doctors, and I would just start crying. My ob-gyn said to me at one point, "Usually, when women cry in my office for no reason, they have postpartum depression."

I shook my head. There was no way I had depression. I had just had another daughter; how could I possibly be depressed? A few days later, we were heading back to church all five of us, the two of us with the three littles in tow. I found myself looking for a seat more toward the middle back of the sanctuary. I found a seat and sat alone. We always sat toward the front. I used to talk to people and engage. I didn't realize at the time what was happening, but others did.

A friend of my husband's asked him one Sunday if I was okay. He said I seemed to be different, not myself. My husband told me what he said and then proceeded to tell me that he told him I was fine. I looked up at him from my seat and saw the smile on his face. I shook my head and agreed with him. I was fine. I sat and thought about what my doctor had said, and now this. I know I felt sad. I know I felt anxious a lot and I cried, but that's just me. That's how I am.

I was embarrassed because everyone says how wonderful it is having children and being a mom, but it was hard. I shouldn't feel like this; I've been so blessed. I struggled to spend time with the Lord, which was the hardest. I just couldn't get the time I so desperately needed. I didn't want to tell anyone what I was going through, and honestly, I don't think I fully recognized it. I thought this was just normal.

My husband was called to pursue a new path in life, teaching. The Lord had put this on his heart. At the time, he was working in a warehouse, and he would drive truck for his company as well. He really believed the Lord called him to teach. He worked a full-time and part-time job. He had a lot on his plate. He didn't understand postpartum depression. How could he? I didn't even understand it myself.

After having my third child, I went back to work way too quickly. It had only been a few weeks. But I had my own business, and if I didn't work, then I didn't get paid. It all became too much for me physically and mentally. It was taking a toll on me. My third daughter also developed baby asthma. I have no experience with that at all, and with no family around and my husband working third shift and going to school, it was incredibly challenging.

One particular night, my daughter was having trouble breathing. I started to get very fearful. I called my husband, but he was already all the way at work. My other two babies were seven and five, and they were both sleeping upstairs. I was in a situation I never wanted to be in, and I had to make a choice. I'm sure we have all been in a situation at one time or another that you never expected or wanted to be in. I called the ambulance, and when they came, I made the decision to send my oldest in the ambulance with my baby because I didn't want her to be alone.

I followed in my car with my middle daughter. We couldn't all go in the ambulance, and I didn't have anyone to stay home and watch the girls. So I followed the ambulance to the hospital. If any of you are alone raising kids with family that is far away, you will understand the anxiety of making decisions alone. I wasn't alone. The Lord was with me, but I found I was just having to make decisions and I wanted someone physically to be there with me.

I know God was with us. He always is. Whether I made the right decisions at the right time or not, God was there covering it all. *Psalm 3:3* reads, *"But you, Lord, are a shield around me."* Olivia received her treatment, and we all met at the hospital. We were all together safe. But that impacted me. The feeling of being alone making these decisions filled me with anxiety. It brings me back to when we got in the accident and the separation anxiety I felt back then. You would think after these situations happen and they are over, you would be relieved and fine. But that's not the case, at least not for me. I carried it all inside. Trying to hold it all together, not letting my feelings show, I believe that attributed to my panic attacks. It was like you can only hold things together for so long before they manifest themselves in some way.

John 14:27 says, *"Peace I leave with you, my peace I give you. I do not give to you as the world gives. Do not let your hearts be troubled and do not be afraid."*

I was thirty-four years old when I had my third daughter. After I had my daughter, I went through the process of finding a new doctor. When I found a new doctor, we had to go through all my family medical history. When she heard my family history, she was concerned about the heart attack my biological father had. I believe that was also attributing to my fear and anxiety.

My doctor wanted to be proactive. She started me on fish oil daily, against my better judgment, I don't like taking medicine if I don't have to. I went to the local store and bought some. Within a week, I began to break out in a rash. I never thought too much about it until a friend of mine noticed and asked me about it. I shrugged it off and didn't think much of it. A few days later, while I was at the gym, someone else had noticed the rash. It had gone from my legs and began to spread across my neck. They suggested I have it checked out.

When I got in the car, I started to get a little nervous and immediately went to the pharmacy. There, I was instructed to go to the doctor's or to a Redi-Med. I started to drive toward home, and that's when I had my first panic attack. As irrational as they are, as you may or may not know, they are very real in the moment.

I started to feel dizzy, my heart started racing, and I was having trouble seeing and breathing. I thought I was going to die. I pulled over and called my husband, panicking, and told him how I felt. I was only five minutes from home, but I decided to turn my car around and pull into the fire station instead. It was closer. They saw the rash, hooked me right up with allergy meds, and brought me straight to the hospital.

This began a five-year downhill spiral. Fear of dying began to grip me. My doctor wanting to be proactive with me constantly swirled around in my mind. Anytime I felt my heart flutter, anytime I felt like I was having a reaction to food, anytime I felt light-headed—anytime I felt anything, I immediately thought, *Is this it? Am I dying?* Then, panic would set in.

A panic attack can present itself the same way as a heart attack. My poor husband, I would call him to check in. I would tell him what I was feeling; he would talk me through it. He would help me breathe, help me figure out if I had felt this way before, and would remind me that I was going to be okay. Looking back, it was a spiritual attack. Unfortunately, we were at a church that didn't really understand or fully take part in all aspects of the power of prayer.

What was going on was a spiritual battle, and I needed spiritual warfare. I needed people to fight for me and with me. In *2 Timothy 1:7 (NKJV)*, it says, *"God has not given us a spirit of fear but of power, love, and a sound mind."* I was gripped by fear. Fear is not from the Lord. *John 10:10* says, *"The thief comes only to steal and kill and destroy, I have come that they may have life, and have it to the full."* Fear had crept in and was destroying me.

In *Isaiah 41:10*, it says, *"So do not fear, for I am with you; do not be dismayed, for I am your God. I will strengthen you and help you; I will uphold you with my righteous right hand."*

1 Peter 1:3–4 NLT

All praise to God the Father of our Lord Jesus Christ. It is by his great mercy that we have been born again, because God raised Jesus Christ from the dead, now we live with great expectation, and we have a priceless inheritance—an inheritance that is kept in heaven for you, pure and undefiled, beyond the reach of change and decay.

My father passed away in August in his early fifties from a heart attack. My father-in-law passed away in July. My youngest was born a month before he passed. We were in the hospital at the same time my father-in-law was admitted. With both fathers passing away right after my daughter's birth, it was hard. How do you celebrate the birth of a child at the same time you grieve the loss of parents? Somehow, you do it. It's this life we live. This imperfect life.

When my father passed away from a heart attack, I remember hearing about his passing from my stepsister. She called to tell me because she knew if she didn't, I wouldn't have known. When I moved out of his house so many years before, we had an on-and-off relationship. I remember going to his funeral. My sister and I went together. When we got there, we stood at the back of the line.

A family member approached us at the funeral home and told us to move to the front of the line. We didn't feel comfortable with that, but she insisted. She told us it was our father and that's where we belonged. Reluctantly, we walked to the front of the line. However, when we got there, we were not allowed to stay. No room for us was made. We were told by other members of the family that our place was at the back of the line. Understanding, we moved back again. As the service went on, a lot of friends from my church came as a support. Even though we had an intermittent relationship, he was still my father.

Toward the end of the service, my stepsister approached us again and asked us to speak. She had felt bad about what had happened and wanted to give us an opportunity to eulogize our biological father. The Spirit inside me jumped. I looked at my sister, and she was shaking her head no. I, however, looked at my stepsister; and before I realized it, I had said yes.

The next thing I knew, she introduced me as the next speaker. It all happened so fast. As I walked toward the front, I began praying and asking the Lord to give me the words I needed. I had not planned this, I had nothing prepared, but I was trusting and following the leading of the Holy Spirit. I honestly don't remember everything. What I do remember was the specific words the Lord put on my heart to share. "I know I didn't get to spend all the time here on earth with my father that I would have liked to. We didn't have the perfect father/daughter relationship. Even though we missed out on our time here on earth, I know the time here is fleeting."

I continued, "My father had given his life to Christ, so I look forward to spending eternity with him in heaven. So many had their time with him here on earth, but I look forward to spending eternity with him in heaven! That is the promise we have!" I praise and thank the Lord for giving me the opportunity to share.

"But our citizenship is in heaven. And we eagerly await a savior from there, the Lord Jesus Christ, who, by the power that enables him to bring everything under his control, will transform our lowly bodies so that they will be like his glorious body" (Philippians 3:20–21).

A few weeks after his funeral, his wife reached out to me and asked me to meet her for lunch. It was there that she told me, "Even though he didn't see you much, I wanted you to know he always loved you."

Jeremiah 1:19

"They will fight against you, but will not overcome you, for I am with you and will rescue you," declares the Lord.

The Lord began to place it on our hearts, and we began to pray and seek for another church. It was time. I wrestled with it because I didn't want to keep changing churches. Our first church, the one we were married in, we had attended for seventeen years; this one had only been seven.

I wanted to make sure it was the Lord leading us and not just me. I wanted to know why we were leaving. I just didn't want to pick up my family and leave. The Lord answered my prayer, like He always does, but not in the way I expected. While I was in prayer about what to do about church—stay or leave—the Lord simply said to me, "The decision has already been made."

I realized that I had been stressing about a decision that He had already made for us. He had already begun to birth this new season in our lives. A few days later, an old acquaintance reached out to me about a new church that had started in my area. She was thinking of going as well, but she wanted to make sure it was from the Lord. During this time, the girls began to go to a youth group that was about forty-five minutes away. The drive was getting to be too much with school. My friend continued to remind me that the new church in the next town over had a small youth group. The girls were the first to go to that new church. They went to the youth group; and the first time they went, my oldest said, "This is our youth group."

A LIFE WORTH SAVING

Finally, we as a family took a step of faith and went to check it out. The Lord knew what our family needed. He knew I needed to heal. Once we submitted to the process, the Lord brought us to a church where the Spirit flowed a little more freely and the healing process for me began.

My husband and I went the next Sunday with the girls; and when we left, my husband confirmed it to me when he said, "This is the first time I have heard the Lord speak to me in a long time." I know that may sound sad, but he was just being honest and he really sensed that this was the place the Lord would bring us to worship next. I still wasn't too sure. Like I shared earlier, I didn't want to be a church "hopper" and I wanted to make sure it was the Lord. I just couldn't leave until the Lord confirmed it in me personally.

I'm thinking at this time, I may still have some issues with trust. As I prayed for days and weeks relentlessly, I continued to ask the Lord why. What is the reason we were leaving? I felt I needed a reason. I felt like I had to make the decisions. I felt like all the decisions fell on me, although they didn't. The rest of the family were all on board with the move.

As I continued to pray, the Lord spoke to me again. "The decision has been made." This time, I listened. I felt a relief to be able to trust the Lord and follow Him. I never want to make the wrong choice. Unfortunately, I do sometimes. If we are all honest, we all do. We can never make the wrong choice when we listen and follow the Lord.

A few weeks later, while worshipping at this new church, the Lord had begun to minister to me. As the worship team began to sing "I am no longer a slave to fear, I am a child of God," by Jonathan David and Melissa Helser, tears began to flow down my cheeks. The Lord was ministering to my tired and broken soul. The Lord is faithful. The Lord is our healer.

The Lord brought me to a safe place where I could finally share my fear and anxiety without judgment or condemnation, a place where I felt safe to open up and share my deep struggles with other women. I had prayed for a group of women like this, a group of women I could be honest with, a group of women that would not judge but love. It was amazing to be at this new church and to be connected with women that I had known years ago.

After reconnecting with this group, we decided to get together, pray, and do a Bible study. The first night, we had an open and honest time of sharing. What a breath of fresh air. It was refreshing to my soul. My walls came down, and I felt comfortable sharing the struggles I had been going through. We laid hands on each other, prayed, and anointed each other with oil. The sweet fragrance of the Lord Jesus Christ spoke and lived through each of us that night.

The next Sunday at church, the Lord spoke to me again through worship. We were worshipping to the "Lion and the Lamb" by Leeland. The Lord spoke. He reminded me of what He said in *1 John 4:4*, *"He who is in me is greater than he who is in the world."* As the song continued, we sang about how every chain is being broken and the kings and kingdoms of this world will bow down. The Lord revealed to me in such a real way that He is the Lion of Judah. *Revelations 5:5 (ASV)* says, *"Weep no more, behold, the Lion that is from the tribe of Judah the root of David has overcome."*

So often, I think of Jesus as the lamb of God, which He is. *John 1:29* says, *"Behold the lamb of God."* But today, on this day, He was revealing to me that He is also the Lion of Judah. As I continued to worship, the Lord showed me a vision.

In the vision, I was standing. I could see coming toward me something that was Fear and Anxiety. This fear and anxiety was coming toward me. I could see them getting closer to me. As I watch them creep closer, they began to move slower. They seemed to become more cautious, yet they were still coming.

As they continued to get closer, what seemed to me to be just close enough, I could see the Lion of Judea that lives inside of me begin to rise up from within me. He opened His mouth and let out a roar that could be heard in the spiritual realm. Immediately, they, Fear and Anxiety, fell to their knees and bowed down before the Lion, the Lion of Judea, who is living inside of me.

Romans 14:11 says, *"For it is written: 'As surely as I live,' says the Lord, 'every knee will bow before me; every tongue will acknowledge God.'"* Whatever is coming against you, cannot stand in the presence of the

King! They fell to their knees in the presence of the Lord! It seemed like the Lord stopped them right in their tracks. It was like the Lord only allowed them to get so close to me and then that was enough. He wouldn't let them go any further. He rose up from within me to protect me. It was like there was a hedge of protection around me; and they, Fear and Anxiety, had to stop. They weren't permitted to get any closer to me. The Lord wouldn't let them! He showed me that He that is in me is greater than he that is in the world. *First John 4:4 says, "You, dear children, are from God and have overcome them, because the one who is in you is greater than the one who is in the world."*

Exodus 14:14 says, "The Lord will fight for you, you need only to be still." In the vision, I just needed to stand! I just needed to be still! The Lord fought the battle! The Lord is our protector. He is Lord and King. If we know Him, He lives inside of us and He is bigger than anything that comes against us. He will protect us; we just need to stand in the presence of our enemies and trust Him, knowing that He loves us and is fighting for us. *First John 4:15 reads, "If anyone acknowledges that Jesus is the Son of God, God lives in them and they in God."*

As we became more involved in the church over the years, the Lord spoke to me and gave me a word, a scripture, to share. I hadn't known this fully yet, but the building the church had been in used to house another church. Something happened, and that church had dissipated. There was some question about housing the new church in the same building that the people were now gathering in.

Praying one day in my devotional time, the Lord spoke to me through His scriptures. He had me read the scripture over and over again. As I did, my soul was encouraged. He then placed it on my heart to share with the pastor's wife. I really hadn't moved in that way in a while, and as I shared with my husband, he was happy to see the Lord use me in that capacity again. This is the scripture the Lord placed on my heart to share.

> *"Who is left among you who saw this temple in its former glory? And how do you see it now? Does it not seem to you like nothing in comparison? But now take*

> *courage, Zerubbabel," declares the Lord, "take courage also, Joshua son of Jehozadak, the high priest, and all you people of the land take courage," declared the Lord, "and work, for I am with you," declares the Lord of Hosts. "As for the promise which I made you when you came out of Egypt, my spirit is abiding in your midst, do not fear!" For thus says the Lord of hosts, "once more in a little while I am going to shake the heavens and the earth, the sea also and the dry land, I will shake all the nations and they will come with the wealth of all nations, and I will fill this house with glory," says the Lord of host. The silver is Mine and the gold is Mine," declare the Lord of hosts. "The latter glory of this house will be greater than the former." Says the Lord of host "and in this place, I will give peace," declares the Lord of hosts. (Hag. 2:3–9 AMP)*

"The latter glory of this house will be greater than the former. And in this place, I will give peace." The Lord used that scripture to encourage and to give peace in the hearts of some that had known of the former.

A life worth saving. Why was my life a life worth saving? When we seek God, and in those times of obedience, He will bring hope, encouragement, and peace to others in Christ through His word that never changes. His word is the same yesterday and today and forever.

Hebrews 13:8 says, *"Jesus Christ is the same yesterday and today and forever."* Later, I was asked to give a testimony on an upcoming Sunday. We were going to be away, so I declined. I was asked a few more times, but because I was going to be away, I again declined. I was encouraged to video my testimony and send. I prayed and was led to share the vision the Lord had given me about fear and anxiety and the freedom in Christ we have if we just stand in the presence of the Lord.

Paul writes in *Philippians 4:1*, *"Therefore, my brothers and sisters, you whom I love and long for, my joy and crown, stand firm in the Lord in this way, dear friends."*

1 John 4:16–18

And so, we know and rely on the love God has for us. God is love, whoever lives in love lives in God, and God in them. This is how love is made complete among us so that we will have confidence on the day of judgment: In this world we are like Jesus. There is no fear in love. But perfect love drives out fear because fear has to do with punishment. The one who fears is not made perfect in love.

All the fear I was carrying was not love. I had acknowledged Jesus. I had given my life to Christ. But where was my love? I began to learn a little about this love when I had my third daughter. As I tried to raise her like I did my other daughters, it was fruitless. I didn't understand what was happening.

When I would speak to her, she wouldn't answer. When I would ask her to do something, I couldn't tell if she heard and understood. She would sometimes shake her head but then would move forward without doing it. Could she not hear me? Could she not understand me? I remember yelling at her one day out of frustration, and she just froze. *"Lord, what is going on?"* I wondered.

I reached out to the pediatrician. When we entered the doctor's office for the visit, she noticed that my daughter had climbed on the chair multiple times and didn't really respond in a way that she would expect when speaking to her. We were encouraged to schedule some testing. We found out that she could hear, but the way she processed the information was different. Sometimes, I would struggle wondering if she was having trouble hearing me or if she was having trouble understanding me.

Early intervention was called, and she had physical therapy and occupational therapy. We went to Boston to have all the testing done, and when all the testing was done, we found that she had an audio-processing disorder. She lacked the skills to interpret her surroundings. Communication was a struggle.

There was one day I remember clearly. I was struggling to communicate; she was struggling to understand. It seemed like she was shutting down. I remember coming down the stairs with tears in my eyes. I was at a complete loss. I remember getting to the bottom of the stairs, and I just fell to my knees, right in the middle of our entryway. I cried out to the Lord. As I knelt on the floor crying out to God, I heard the Lord speak the word *love*.

I sat there as He began to stir in my heart *to love*. As I sat in His presence, I began to sink down deeper into the floor as I heard Him tell me, "Love her."

In that moment, honesty came bubbling to the surface. As I sobbed, I realized, "Lord, I don't know how to love. Lord, teach me, show me, help me to love." What a humbling moment. As sad as that moment was to me, it was a turning point in my life and a chance for more healing to take place.

If we can't be real with God, who can we be real with? I asked the Lord to show me, to fill me with His love so I could fully love. *First John 4:19* says, *"We love because he first loved us."* Unconditional love. What is that? Unconditional love, known as affection without any limitations or love without conditions. I remember my oldest daughter telling me she felt like my love was conditional.

I began a journey to learn love, true love. I am beginning to understand more and more. God's love is agape love; this is the highest form of love. The Lord is showing me. He is teaching me. *First John 4:16 (ESV)* says, *"So we have come to know and to believe the love that God has for us. God is love…and whoever abides in love abides in God, and God abides in him."* I feel like I should know this already, but I don't.

This is and will be a lifelong process for me. Love. What is love? How do I love?

> *For this reason, I kneel before the Father, from whom every family in heaven and on earth derives its name. I pray that from His glorious riches he may strengthen you with power through His Spirit in your inner being, so that Christ may dwell in your hearts through faith. And I pray that you, being rooted and established in love, may have power, together with all the Lord's holy people to grasp how wide and long and high and deep is the love of Christ and to know this love that surpasses knowledge—that you may be filled to the measure of all the fullness of God. (Eph. 3:14–21)*

The Lord put it on my heart to use calligraphy and write *1 Corinthians 13:4–5* on the stairs to our second floor: *"Love is patient, love is kind, it does not envy, it does not boast, it is not proud, it does not dishonor others, it is not self-seeking it is not easily angered, it keeps no records of wrongs."* It was written as a reminder to me how to love.

John 11:35

―∞―

Jesus Wept.

This year, I have come to realized that I may lack the ability to feel. To feel deeply, that is. Don't get me wrong; I can feel anger, overwhelming sadness, and even bursts of happiness. But now at forty-five, I have come to the conclusion that I truly lack the ability to feel. What does that even mean?

My daughter lost a friend this year. A mom and father lost a daughter, a brother lost his sister. Many lost a friend. When I first heard the news, it was from my middle daughter. She simply sent me this text: "I'm too emotional to go to practice today." As a mom, well this mom, those aren't words I usually hear from my fifteen-year-old. I reached out to her until I was able to get all the information I was lacking.

I was told a friend of my oldest daughter had passed away from complications to a pretty "normal" sickness. My first thought went to my oldest. Why hadn't I heard from her? I knew how close my oldest daughter was to her, and I was concerned. They played volleyball together, and they had talked about going on a mission's trip together in the upcoming year. I reached out to my daughter.

When I was able to get in touch with her, she informed me that her school had called her class down and had a meeting at the school and she had been in the gym. She had been there this whole time, grieving the loss. What a devastating loss for so many. Parents received a call, letting us all know that all practices had been canceled as well as all after-school activities. To be honest, initially, that response was confusing to me. Why would the school cancel all the programs?

I realized I had subconsciously been taught my whole life that you don't feel; you just move on. I wasn't taught to grieve. I wasn't taught to process or feel loss. This response from the school was appropriate, yet it was very new to me. For something as simple as me being sick when I was younger, I was never allowed to stay home. I was always told to get up, take some medicine, and go to school. I was programmed to just keep moving.

When I had my third child, I went back to work after a couple weeks. I wasn't ready. I could feel it in my body that I wasn't ready, but I put her in the carrier and took her with me anyway. That's just what I thought was the right thing to do. I remember my body (emotionally, physically, and spiritually) screaming at me, *It's too much!* But I kept moving. I never took the time to rest. I never took the time to reflect on sadness or on joy. It's tragic how some of us don't allow ourselves our basic physical, emotional, and spiritual needs. After my third child, it took me over a year to heal. It took over a year before I felt like my body was right again.

That is much different than losing someone. However, learning to listen, learning to feel is so very important. I had lost my father, my stepfather, my baby. I never fully processed through the pain of those losses. That's where the anxiety comes in. I think that's where anger and outbursts come into play for people who don't know how to process—bouts of tears and sadness, it's all unhealthiness. I needed to learn to process and feel. This was the beginning of my year to feel.

The response to the loss of this child began. It was like we were given the time to grieve and we were given the okay to stop and process this loss as a people and as a community. We were allowed to stop, feel the sadness, feel the pain, feel the loss. This was new for me, and as I thought about my oldest, I knew I needed to pray and be there for her.

Praise God if you learned and learned well! Some of us do what is healthy by instinct, and some of us need our eyes to be opened along the way. There were instances in my past I would start to feel, but something was said or done that would directly impact me and the grieving process was stifled. I was taught and raised the way the previous generation was taught and raised, and so on and so on. With humility and grace, we can allow the Lord to show us a new way, and that is what I believe began to happen in me.

I saw so much love through this time in our family and in our town. I saw friends stand with friends, parents supporting and comforting young adults. As we sat at the calling hours and the funeral, what I saw was beautiful. I saw comforting gentle gestures all around, whether it was a reassuring hand on someone's back, letting them know they weren't alone, or a hand on a knee or a hand met with a gentle squeeze. I saw example after example of love. I sat with my daughter, took the time to be there for her and watched her be a comfort to her friends. I saw my daughter receive prayer at church. The spiritual and emotional protection our pastor and friends showed as they gathered around her in love, was a true example of Christ's love.

I saw a place that overwhelmed my soul. To witness love, unconditional love, was and is beautiful. As I sat and watched all this unfold around me, the Lord was showing me something. He was showing me true love. He was showing me peace, a deeper peace than I had never known, one that I had been seeking.

I saw a safe place. I found a safe place in the Father's arms through a very difficult time. I saw Christ's love emerge. I watched as God's hand moved all around through the kids, through the priests, through the pastors, and through the parents. Amazing love, amazing grace through such a difficult time. It made me stop and open my eyes to see the healing in the feeling process, the process of feeling sadness, of feeling loss. What a powerful thing.

I encourage you to take the time to rest. Take the time to process. Take the time to heal. For in it and through it, you will see the love of Christ emerge. Embrace it. What I was lacking was the ability to feel, which in turn inhibited my growth, inhibited my ability to heal, and inhibited my ability to give and receive grace. Amazing grace, the grace that can only come from the One.

Let us then approach God's throne of grace with confidence, so that we may receive mercy and find grace to help us in our time of need. (Heb. 4:16)

Galatians 2:20

I have been crucified in Christ and I no longer live but Christ lives in me. The life I now live in the body, I live by faith in the Son of God, who loved me and gave himself up for me.

After settling in and becoming part of this new church, we engaged in outreach ministry, children's ministry, youth ministry, women's ministry, and the worship team. It was a small church, so we jumped in and helped wherever needed. We knew the Lord would sort it all out. After a couple years, I was asked to be one of the breakout speakers at the church's upcoming women's conference. The scripture that was given by the pastor's wife for the conference was *Galatians 2:20*. *"I have been crucified in Christ and I no longer live but Christ lives in me. The life I now live in the body, I live by faith in the Son of God, who loved me and gave himself up for me."*

As I began to seek the Lord, my mind was swirling a bit. I continued to pray, and the only thing that kept coming to my mind was a question. Who am I in Christ? I felt the Lord stop my mind from swirling as I really began to settle in on that question. *Who really am I in Christ?* I thought, *Lord, where have I come from, who was I, and where am I today because of who you are?*

While I continued to seek the Lord, He led me to a book that was on my nightstand. The book was by Kay Arthur, and it was entitled *Lord I Want to Know You*. As I began praying, the Lord spoke to me and said, "In order to know who you are in Christ, you must first know me." Profound, isn't it? So who really is God? Will we ever really fully be able to know God? This is my journey, this is our journey—to fully know Him.

My identity was in Christ, but who am I really and who is Christ? The Lord began to lay the names of God upon my heart. Who am I, who is Christ, and who am I in Christ? What's my identity? Here are six of them

El Roi, the God of seeing

This was the name ascribed to God by Hagar when she was alone and desperate. In the wilderness, Hagar describes that she met "the God that sees." She had been driven out by Sarah, and when Hagar met the angel of the Lord, she realized she had seen God Himself. She also realized that He is a God who sees her and loves her.

The Lord sees me, He saw me at the beginning of life. He saw me in the middle, and He saw all I had gone through, and He sees me now. He even wept for me. The whole time, He saw me. He had a plan that He had put in place for me.

> *She gave this name to the Lord who spoke to her, "You are God who sees me," for she said, "I have now seen the One who sees me." (Gen. 16:13)*

Yahway-Shammah, the Lord is there

> *And the name of the city from that time on will be: THE LORD IS THERE.*
>
> —Ezekiel 48:35

> *My dwelling place will be with them; I will be their God, and they will be my people. (Ezekiel 37:27)*

All those times in my life that I felt alone, God was there. I wasn't alone. He was there. He never left me. In His great wisdom and in His perfect timing, He brought me from place to place. He never left. He was always there.

El-Elyon, the Most High God

Do not fear the enemy who tried to intimidate you; know that your God is the Most High God.

In all those times in my life when I felt gripped with fear, when the enemy tried to intimidate me, the Lord, the Most High was there fighting those battles for me. He fights those battles for you as well.

> *For you, Lord. Are the Most High over all the earth; you are exalted far above all gods. (Psa. 97:9)*

Eloah Selichot, the God of forgiveness

Who is God? He is the God of forgiveness. I have made many mistakes—we all have—yet He has forgiven them all. He does not leave us in our wretchedness. In His great mercy, He brings them to the light and offers us forgiveness through His Son. I am forgiven.

> *But you are a forgiving God, gracious and compassionate, slow to anger and abounding in love. Therefore you did not desert them. (Neh. 9:17)*

Yahwey-M-Kaddesh, the Lord who sanctifies, makes holy

You, Lord, are holy. Moses took off his shoes in your presence because in your presence, he was standing on holy ground. *Exodus 3:5* reads, *"Take off your sandals, for the place where you are standing is holy ground."* He sent His Son to sanctify us that we may sit and bask in His beautiful presence, in His holiness. Jesus's blood was shed so our sins would be covered so that we may enter into His presence and have relationship with Him.

A LIFE WORTH SAVING

Yahweh-Rapha, the Lord who heals

Psalm 30:2 reads, "Lord my God, I called to you for help, and you healed me." Jesus has healed me; and He continues to heal me emotionally, physically, and spiritually.

May faith continue to rise within that I may not forget what you have done. *Psalm 103:2–5 says, "Praise the Lord, my soul; all my inmost being, praise his holy name. Praise the Lord, my soul. And forget not all his benefits—who forgives all your sins and heals all your diseases, who redeems your life from the pit and crowns you with love and compassion, who satisfies your desires with good things."*

Who am I in Christ? You would think the answer would be bold and strong, and I guess it is, but not in a way that may first come to mind. Let me share a picture that I saw. For me, this picture sums up my life with Jesus, and it gives me peace. It's a picture of a Lion, His face turned up toward the heavens. The sun's warmth is surrounding, shining down. Underneath, snuggled secure to His chest, is a little girl. Her arms wrap around His, His paws protecting her.

Her eyes are closed. She is resting at peace—Shalom—because she knows her Father has her. As she is nestled in close, she is covered. She is sheltered. She is protected, and she is loved. That little girl is a picture of me. It's a picture of us all if we let it be. *Ps 91:1–2 says, "Whoever dwells in the shelter of the Most high will rest in the shadow of the Almighty. I will say of the lord, 'He is my refuge and my fortress, my God in whom I trust.'"*

I am safe in the arms of the Father, and so are you. Piece by piece, layer by layer, I am being crucified by Christ. It is no longer I that live but Christ that lives in me. *First Corinthians 14:25 says, "As the secrets of their hearts are laid bare. So, they will fall down and worship God, exclaiming, 'God is really among you!'"*

Share your heart with the Lord. Tell Him your secrets. He knows them anyway. As we lay our secrets bare before Him, as we bring them to the light, God begins to do His work in us and then we can say, "It is no longer I that live but Christ that lives in me."

Who am I in Christ?

> *The Spirit of the Sovereign Lord is on me,*
> *Because the Lord has anointed me to proclaim*
> *Good news to the poor*
> *He has sent me to bind up the broken hearted.*
> *To proclaim freedom for the captives and*
> *Release from darkness for the prisoners,*
> *To proclaim the year of the Lord's favor and the day of*
> *vengeance of our God,*
> *To comfort all who mourn,*
> *And provide for those who grieve in Zion—*
> *To bestow on them a crown of beauty instead of ashes*
> *The oil of joy instead of mourning, and a garment of*
> *praise instead of despair,*
> *They will be called oaks of righteousness,*
> *A planting of the Lord for the display of His splendor.*
> *(Isa. 61:1–3)*

Who am I in Christ?

In order to know who we are in Christ, we must first know Christ. Rest in Him, submit to Him, kneel before Him, allow Him to be Lord of your life. Let Him do all the work He needs to do within you, through you, and in your life. Trust in Him, and little by little, we will begin to be transformed into the image of Christ.

Psalm 44:3 says, *"It is not by their sword that they won the land, nor did their arm bring them victory; it was your right hand, your arm, and the light of your face, for you loved them."*

Matthew 7:7

Ask and it will be given to you; seek and you will find; knock and the door will be open to you.

When we moved from one town to another, we settled into our house fairly quickly and our children started their new school. The minute we moved in, we realized that the house really wasn't any bigger than the house we left, we noticed right away but made it work. I had always thought about foster care, and as time went on, the Lord began to place it on our hearts more and more.

We started taking the classes necessary to become foster parents. We were approved, and the next phase of our lives took root. With the added person in our house and the addition of a dog, we were feeling the space shrink. We began to pray again. As I prayed, I felt the Lord pressing on my heart to put our house on the market. Even though this had been on my heart for a while and I felt as though the Lord was in it, I was concerned.

I remember going to my husband and questioning how this was all going to work out. We had a foster daughter, plus our three girls, as well as Max our golden retriever. "Lord, where are we supposed to go?" I began praying and asking the Lord for faith. That's a lot of people to be responsible for. I asked God to show me something, anything that would help me know that we would be okay. I was concerned about the logistics of everyone and everything. What would we do when our house was sold? Where would we go? We couldn't move into an apartment with all these people and all this stuff.

About a month after we began to seek the Lord about another move, we received an invitation to listen to an old friend speak at a place just a few towns away. We had known him for years; we had even served together in youth ministry in our younger years. We decided to go. While we were there, we noticed another couple that we had known for years, and we went over and sat with them. It's so great to be in a community of believers. You always pick up right where you left off. The bond of the family of Christ is like no other.

As we sat together, we began to share what the Lord had been doing in our lives. We shared how the Lord had put it on our hearts to become foster parents, and now, we believed he was stirring us to sell our house. I laughed as I told them that I told God that He needed to help us out here; we had a lot of people we were responsible for. I told Him I kind of needed a plan before we could make such a big move with all these lives!

They looked at each other then at us in disbelief. They began to share with us how the people that had been renting their house were moving out and they had been praying that they would find new renters. The Lord is always so good! Immediately, I began thanking the Lord for answered prayers. We went home and put our house on the market. The house sold almost immediately. When the Lord says to move, He moves!

We moved into their house and began renting while we search for another house. The house was in the next town over but would be the same district for high school. I have children, so there were some hiccups. My youngest daughter told her teacher that we had moved to another town. She didn't understand that we were still in the same district but different middle schools. I received a phone call from the school telling us we needed to take the kids out and they needed to change schools. We prayed and put a call into the principal. He told us the kids could stay until the end of the year, but if we didn't find a house in the district by the beginning of the next year, the younger girls would have to change middle schools.

As time went by, it was very tough for my husband. He had worked his whole life, and to now be renting a house from someone else was not the best financial plan. As each month went by, it got harder and harder for him knowing our money was going to something that wasn't ours. We looked all around and couldn't find anything. Then, something an old friend told me years ago came to my mind. She told me that when she and her family were buying a house, they made a list of things they wanted. To me, that didn't make sense.

I remember thinking at the time how selfish that sounded. That didn't sit well with me, and I couldn't figure out why the Lord would remind me of that. I felt like that wasn't being thankful. I felt like we should be thankful for anything the Lord chose to give us. Whenever I prayed about the move, my friend's voice would come to my mind over and over again, "Make a list."

Finally, I submitted. "Okay, I'm going to ask the family what they want in a house, and I will make a list. But the list will only be in my head." *John 16:24 (ESV)* says, *"Until now you have asked for nothing in My name; ask and you will receive, so that your joy may be made full."* I humbly gave the list verbally to the Lord. I still had trouble asking God for what I wanted, but I submitted to His will for us. If it's His will, then I will trust Him, knowing that whatever He chose to give us would be a blessing and would be enough.

Shortly after I verbally shared my list with the Lord, we found the house! It had all we wanted, all that we asked for. We knew it was ours. When we saw the house for the first time, each daughter went through and picked their room. Although it needed some updating, it was in our price range and it had all we had asked for. We put in the offer. Within a few days, we found out that our offer was rejected and the sellers had gone with another buyer. How could that be? We knew that this was our house. Immediately, my husband and I looked at each other, and we knew somehow this was going to be our home. We had peace knowing that, somehow, the house would become available again.

We went on with our lives in faith without worry, knowing the Lord had a plan and He was growing our faith. About a month later, my husband was looking through the real estate online and saw that the house was up for sale again! We knew it! It was about midnight, but I was so excited that I immediately texted our realtor anyway and told her we wanted to put in an offer again.

She was up working late, and to my surprise, she texted me back within minutes. She told us she would write up the offer again and present it to them the next morning. The house fell through because the buyers were concerned about the pool, so they backed out. We got the house! The Lord met us where we were, and He provided us with even more than what we had asked for. Not only did it have a basketball hoop, four bedrooms, two bathrooms, and an in-ground pool; but the property was also lined with a beautiful white fence. We would be able to let out our Max, our golden retriever, and he would be safe to roam freely in our backyard. It was a blessing!

Proverbs 1:32–33

For the waywardness of the simple will kill them, and the complacency of fools will destroy them, but whoever listens to me will live in safety and be at ease without fear of harm.

These last chapters once again show the grace and mercy of a loving Father to a daughter who questions all things every time, even to her own detriment. When will she learn? When will any of us learn?

We see love in human form, an imperfect form. We have a God who loves and cares for us in perfect form. We have a Father that loves us unconditionally, a Father that wants to protect us. Yet we continue to live our lives like we are alone. We live like we have to make all these decisions all on our own, almost like turning our backs on the One who wants to protect us the most. He protects out of His love for us.

Do we know more than God? When will I learn? We have a Father unlike any we have known here on earth—a God who pursues us, a God who speaks to us. Do we listen? We have a God who wants to protect us. He's a Father that sees. He longs for relationship. He longs for His children to know Him, to trust Him. He puts His hands out and says, "Trust Me." When will we learn to trust the Lord wholeheartedly and not lean on our own understanding? *Proverbs 3:5–6 says, "Trust in the Lord with all your heart and lean not on your own understanding; in all your ways acknowledge Him, and he will make your paths straight.*

As I sit here typing these last few chapters, I sit alone. It's been a year and a half since the incident. The Lord spoke to me, but it didn't make sense, just like He spoke to me all those years ago in the car. Had I not grown? Had I not grown in twenty years? Was I still needing to learn the same lesson?

> *I do not understand what I do. For what I want to do I do not do, but what I hate I do. And if I do what I do not want to do, I agree that the law is good, as it is, it is no longer I, myself who do it, but it is sin living in me. For I know that good itself does not dwell in me, that is, in my sinful nature. For I have the desire to do what is good, but I cannot carry it out. For I do not do the good I want to do, but the evil I do not want to do—this I keep on doing. Now if I do what I do not want to do, it is no longer I who do it, but it is sin living in me that does it. (Rom. 7:15–20)*

Here is my last story. It is a story of a woman who loves God; yet as Paul said in Romans, I do as I do not want to do. Through this, I am learning and experiencing God's love like never before. I am experiencing God's mercy and grace. I am learning compassion and understanding. I am learning to slow down, to breathe, to trust God.

A few years ago, I saw a house for sale in Vermont. It was everything I have always dreamed of. Since I was younger, I have always wanted to open a home for young pregnant women. I wanted to give them a place, a safe place, they could go to carry out their nine months of pregnancy, a place that would encourage and support them and their baby up until birth and beyond.

When I saw this house, I fell in love with it. I convinced my husband to go in and walk around. I had the same sense I did with the last house we purchased. It felt like ours. It was listed as a bed and breakfast and had the space and everything needed for opening a home for pregnant teens. It was a dream come true. As we talked about it, my husband didn't seem to be on board. So we put it aside for a while. A little while later, my husband brought it up again. He had spoken to some friends, and one wanted to invest and financially support the start-up.

It was exciting, but then, I got nervous. We had two children in college, and I was thinking we needed to wait a few years until they were done. My husband also worked in another state, and we didn't know how all that would work. We talked and dreamed about it for months. I contacted a few people on how to start a nonprofit. We were excited! Could we do this? Was it time? I continued to do research, but we never made the jump. We began to think to wonder, *Was there even a need for something like this anymore?* We put it on the back burner again, but we kept checking on the house every few months. We saw the price go down, and we called the realtor and began to look at it again. It sold before we could move forward.

I felt like that had been something the Lord had put on my heart years ago; it felt like my purpose. Did we wait too long? Did fear get in the way? Was it the wrong timing? As we began to move forward in our lives putting that dream aside, I was disappointed. I began to try to figure out what I was going to do with the next few years of my life. My kids are grown, two are off at college, they don't need me as much. I only work until two thirty; I always had mother's hours.

What was I going to do every day at two thirty? No more meets, no more volleyball matches, no more horse lessons, no more soccer practices, no more youth group two times a week. Lord, what is next for my life? I thought, *Well, maybe I should take this time to start taking care of myself.* I was having some tightness in my chest that had been determined to not be a heart problem. A coworker always talked about his chiropractor and how great he was, so I decided to see him.

I called the doctor and asked for a referral. At first, they told me they don't do referrals to chiropractors, only to physical therapists; but I persisted, telling them he came highly recommended. They put the referral in. I tried to call a couple times with no success. Either they didn't answer the phone, or they didn't have a day or time that worked for me. I wondered, *Maybe I shouldn't go?* It didn't seem to be working out.

I let it go for a few months and then tried again. The call went through, and I made an appointment. As the appointment grew closer, they called and canceled. I thought, *Okay, maybe this chiropractor thing isn't such a good idea.* I hadn't felt the tightness anymore, so was it really necessary? A few months went by, and my coworker was talking about his chiropractor again. I decided to call one more time. I made the appointment for a few weeks out.

The day of the appointment, I wondered again, *Should I go? Why was I going? I hadn't felt the tightness in a while.* I convinced myself to go, thinking he would be able to give me some pointers on my posture and how to avoid the tightness in the future. I reminded myself that it was time to take care of my body, and this was a good way to do it. I had made the appointment; I should just go. On the way to the appointment, I got lost. I started driving around in circles. I finally stopped and prayed.

I sensed I should call my husband; however, I was kind of holding a grudge that day. I don't even remember why, but I decided not to call him. He didn't even know I had made the appointment. I knew he would tell me not to go. *Proverbs 28:14* says, *"Blessed is the one who always trembles before God, but whoever hardens their heart falls into trouble."* I struggled as I prayed. *What's the big deal anyway? I'll be fine*, I thought. As I sat in the car, I felt like maybe I shouldn't go, but I couldn't figure out if it was God or just my anxiety.

I have dealt with fear and anxiety, and sometimes, it's a struggle for me to understand if I'm having anxiety about something or if it's actually the Lord trying to protect me. I decided that I was being silly and I would be fine. So I pushed past it, and I called the office and got directions.

Luke 6:46 says, *"Why do you call me 'Lord, Lord,' and not do what I tell you?"*

1 Thessalonians 5:16–18

Rejoice always, pray continually, give thanks in all circumstances; for this is God's will for you in Christ Jesus.

The day after my chiropractor appointment, when I woke up, I felt like I had been hit by a truck. Getting out of bed was painful. There was something wrong with my neck, and I had a headache that was persistent. I struggled throughout the day but thought it would get better as the day went on.

However, that didn't happen. I went to bed and woke in the middle of the night. I usually do, but this was different. When I got out of bed, I felt dizzy. I found the side of the bed, and I sat down. The next thing I know, I woke up on a hard surface, not knowing where I was. I do remember feeling the cold hard floor underneath me, but I wasn't sure how I had gotten there. I tried to get up but couldn't. I felt my body settle back into the floor again, relieved to feel the coolness of the floor entering my body.

Was I hot? Was I sweating? I must have gone out again or fallen asleep, I'm not quite sure. But when I woke up a little while later, I was still on the floor. I managed to get up and went to my husband. I told him all that happened, but I was now feeling fine. Did it happen? Was I imagining it? He had me get up and walk around a little to see if I felt anything. I didn't feel anything in my body that would cause something like that.

I waited a few more days. My headache persisted, and my neck was not better. We began to wonder if I had whiplash. I called the office to tell them how I was feeling and what had happened a few nights before. They told me sometimes a little discomfort would be normal, and they couldn't explain the rest of what happened. Two weeks went by, and my neck was getting worse. I began having more pain. I called the office again and was told that there must be something else going on and I should call my primary care doctor. A few days later, I called my primary care doctor, but I would have to wait a few weeks to get an appointment. I was told to take Advil and to use cold and heat on my neck.

When I finally had my appointment, my doctor looked at me, and there was significate loss of motion in my neck. My headaches persisted, and there was numbness in my face and neck. She referred me to a neurologist. While I waited for my appointment to see the neurologist, the numbness in my face had continued to go down my neck, then my arm and then my leg. I couldn't lie down to sleep because of the nerve pain on my left side. I tried to sleep in a sitting position, which worked for a little bit, but in time, I started to feel pain down my spine. I was scared.

I finally saw the neurologist, and she ordered an MRI. The results came back, and they were fine. I was not fine. She then ordered a CAT scan. While I was waiting for the tests to come back, I woke up one morning to a ringing in my left ear. I panicked. What was happening to my body? I called my primary care doctor, and she sent me to an ear, nose, and throat doctor. He looked and found nothing that would cause the ringing. He told me that these things sometimes just happen.

As weeks and months passed, physical issues continued to emerge. I started feeling a burning sensation in my neck and chest. I was sent to a pain specialist. He suggested I see a physical therapist. My doctor didn't want to do that until we received the results from the CAT scan. She wanted to make sure there wasn't anything broken in my neck before she sent me to PT. She put me on muscle relaxers. I received the results from my last test from the neurologist. She told me everything came out fine and there was nothing she could do. I was extremely frustrated. I was glad they didn't find anything, yet I knew there was something wrong.

A few weeks later, I was driving to work and was talking on the phone, and all of a sudden, I couldn't swallow! I panicked. I grabbed a bottle of water, and I was able to drink. I went into work and called the doctor. She again sent me to an ENT and a speech therapist. I could swallow most of the time, but there were instances that I found I couldn't, like if I was walking fast or pushing a carriage or carrying something heavy. I found it hard at work because the more I typed, the more it affected my throat, which in turn would affect my swallowing. The doctor took me off the muscle relaxers and put me on some anxiety medicine. I started taking that medicine for a while. Then I started having GI issues. The doctor told me I needed to find another way to deal with the muscles. He told me that being on the anxiety medicine I was on could have some long-term effects that would be even more difficult to manage.

Lord, what is going on! Whiplash, headaches, nerve pain, ringing in my ear, swallowing issues, neck and throat tightness, and now I was having GI problems! I began to cry out to the Lord. My husband and I prayed. I confessed to my husband how I was feeling and how much of a mess up I felt as a Christian. The Lord was trying to protect me. Looking back, I knew He didn't want me to go to the chiropractor. Why didn't I listen? Why didn't I listen to the Lord?

I left the room and went into the shower where I spent the next hour confessing and crying out to the Lord. "Lord, heal me," I prayed. "Lord, forgive me. Help me to swallow. Help me be well." Will I have a future? What kind of future will it be? I thought, *This is the time in our lives that my children are grown, and a new chapter was opening up to us. Why is this happening to me now?*

I knew the Lord had more for us. How would it be possible to be open to do all God would have for us if I'm like this? Through my tears, the Lord spoke, "*Ephesians 3:20–21: 'Now to him who is able to do immeasurable more than all we ask or imagine, according to his power that is at work within us, to him be the glory in the church and in Christ Jesus throughout all generations, forever and ever! Amen.'*" As the scripture came to my mind, I pondered it.

As I spoke it over and over again in my mind, I could see myself whole and happy. I was traveling, staying at a hotel and eating at a restaurant. I haven't eaten in a restaurant in years because of my allergies, and I have always been afraid to fly! I sensed and believed what the Lord was saying to me. He was going to do more for me than I could ever ask or imagine. I was encouraged, and my faith began to be restored.

The next day on my husband's way to work, he heard a song on the radio, and he sent it to me. He felt the Lord nudging him to share it with me. It's by Casting Crowns called "God of All My Days."

This song spoke to my heart. It put all the feelings I was having into words. I didn't feel alone anymore. This song that was sung by a Christ follower felt the same way as me, yet he found comfort in the Lord.

Ephesians 4:15

Instead, speaking the truth in love, we will grow to become in every respect the mature body of him who is the head, that is Christ.

I want to praise and thank God for putting doctors in my life that told me the truth in love. The Lord knew what I needed. The results of my tests came in, and my primary care doctor went over the results. Nothing came up on the CAT scan. I was happy but frustrated at the same time. As I spoke, I started to get emotional; worry set in.

My doctor stopped me, looked me in the eye, and said, "You are beginning to worry me. Most people come in, hear the treatment plan, and move forward. You, however, are going down a path that I don't like." She spoke to me in faith. She spoke to me about thankfulness. She asked me a series of questions. "Can you walk? Can you get yourself ready in the morning? Can you go to work?" She then asked if I drove to the office that day. I responded yes to all.

She looked right at me again and said, "Then you should be thankful. You need to wake up every morning and thank the Lord for all the things that you can do." A thankful heart is what changes everything. *Proverbs 17:22* says, *"A cheerful heart is good medicine, but a crushed spirit dries up the bones."* She encouraged me to focus on all the things that I could do. She encouraged me to begin to be thankful every day and to move forward in faith. *Philippians 4:6–7 says, "Do not be anxious about anything, but in every situation, by prayer and petition with thanksgiving, present your request to God; and the peace of God, which transcends all understanding, will guard your hearts and your minds in Christ Jesus."*

I had seen another doctor, and he spoke the truth in love as well. He shared with me about two women who had swallowing issues. Both had been on medication. One was able to get off; one was not. The difference between the two was one sought yoga, meditation, and personal faith. The other did not. I felt the Lord speaking to me as the doctor encouraged me to seek out alternatives to long-term medication. He was concerned about the potential lasting effects they would have.

My physical therapist who was working on my throat and neck muscles also encouraged me to wean off the muscle relaxers. He explained that when an injury occurs, there often becomes a weak spot in our body. For that reason, if I'm sick, stressed, or excited, my body would find that weak spot. He told me that medicine is okay to take as needed, but during the process of healing, he didn't want the medicine to inhibit the work he was performing on my muscles.

It's funny that I've always been against medicine, but through this time, the Lord allowed me to grasp a deeper understanding of its need. The Lord is the ultimate doctor who works through people in the medical field to add support to the health and healing process when we need it. The Lord gave me more compassion for those who, through trauma or unforeseen circumstances, had been given medicine and found themselves in a cycle of dependency. I'm thankful for the doctors who, at the right time, helped me navigate the potential dependency by sharing with me the truth in love.

I had been reading and praying my whole life. Sometimes, though, it would seem like stress praying. I needed to learn to rest, to trust. Writing and journaling was too much in the morning, so every morning, I began opening the Bible app. I simply read the verse of the day, turned on the background music that was in the prayer app, and I began to meditate on the scripture. Every day, I opened the Bible app, turned on the volume, and I quietly read and meditated on the daily guided prayer. I was breathing in the breath of life as I spent time meditating on the Lord. *Job 33:4* says, *"The Spirit of God has made me. And the breath of the Almighty gives me life."*

1 John 4:18

There is no fear in Love. But perfect love drives out all fear because fear has to do with punishment. The one who fears is not made perfect in Love.

I had a choice between two physical therapists. One was in the city where there would be better, more equipped medical professionals. The other was in the small town I worked in. I was tired. I was tired of traveling and seeing so many doctors. "Lord, I trust You. No matter where I go, I know You will be with me, guiding me."

I decided to stick with the small-town physical therapist that was in the small hospital in town. I was happy to finally move forward, and I was looking forward to some kind of recovery. My first visit was just an intake. The physical therapist had me lie down, and she started to work on my neck. As she moved my neck, I immediately felt my throat restrict and I struggled to swallow. She stopped and consulted with another physical therapist.

When she came back, she told me she was going to reschedule me with a different physical therapist. She explained to me that one of the other therapists had more knowledge, and she was more comfortable with me seeing her. I made another appointment and returned in a few days. When I met the new physical therapist, she looked at me and explained that she wasn't equipped to treat my injury either but she knew someone who would be.

She explained that she could work on the outside muscles; however, in doing so, it was restricting my inner muscles. She explained that she was not trained to treat those deep-tissue muscles. She gave me the number to another physical therapist who she had worked with before. He was about an hour away, but he was highly trained and actually taught others. He specialized in nerves and the deep-tissue muscles that were attached to my spine. When I left, I felt encouraged and hopeful! *Jeremiah 29:11* says, *"For I know the plans I have for you, declare the Lord, plans to prosper you and not to harm you, plans to give you hope and a future."*

My husband went with me to that first physical therapy appointment. It had been about an hour away, and I didn't want to go alone. Before we went in, we took the time to pray. We were both encouraged. I was feeling like we were finally moving forward, and I was looking forward to getting the help I needed. *First Peter 5:10* says, *"And the God of all grace, who called you to his eternal glory in Christ, after you have suffered a little while, will himself restore you and make you strong, firm and steadfast."* The Lord had a plan and a path for me, and I was beginning to see it play out.

When we walked in the building, the first thing we saw was a statue of Jesus. As I turned, I could see the scriptures on the wall. *Okay, Lord. What are You doing here?* I thought. As we sat in the waiting room, I could softly hear in the background Christian music playing. *"Lord, You are good."* When my name was called, I began to feel a little hesitant. The thought of another doctor working on me made me nervous considering what I was going through. Trust would take some time.

As I sat in the room waiting for the physical therapist, it was quiet and I tried to focus on the Christian music playing. I prayed. The first person I saw did an intake. I explained all the symptoms I was having, and he looked right at me and said, "That all makes sense."

I looked at him in bewilderment. "It does?" I asked. He began to explain the path of my nerves and explained that the tightness or inflammation from whiplash would affect my nerves. He explained that the neurologist wouldn't see it because she is only looking for breaks or fractures. The nerve path from my neck injury would run in the format I was describing: headaches, facial numbness, ringing in the ear, throat issues, arm and leg numbness, and it could follow all the way to the GI track.

My eyes started to water as he spoke. Finally, someone who knows this is not all in my head! Someone who knows and understands! The next half hour was spent with the owner. He worked on my nerves as well as my neck. When I left the office, I went to the car and got in. I sat there awhile, overwhelmed by the goodness of God, unable to speak. Tears began to flow in response to the relief I was feeling. My husband, not knowing why I was crying, kept asking me what was wrong. He seemed concerned. When I was able to compose myself, I shared with him how the Lord led me to this place. I began to weep full of thankfulness, full of hope. I sat praising and thanking the Lord for bringing me to this place. *Psalm 42:11* says, *"Why, my soul, are you downcast? Why so disturbed within me? Put your hope in God, for I will yet praise him, my Savior and my God."*

I began going to physical therapy two times a week for the next year and a half. During that time, the Lord worked on my body, soul, and spirit. I was taught to breathe. I had been breathing in my chest for years, which was causing more tightening of the muscles in my neck and my throat. I was taught to slow down. When I was having difficulty swallowing, I was taught to focus on my breathing. Some days, I would come in a mess, worried and frustrated. Other days, I would come in filled with hope.

One time, when I was feeling frustrated and fearful, I shared how I felt I would never get well. As the physical therapist worked on me, he asked, "What is the opposite of fear?" I was quiet I didn't know. "Love," he said. "If your full of fear, there's no room for love." *First John 4:18 says, "There is no fear in love, but perfect love drives out fear, because fear has to do with punishment. The one who fears is not made perfect in love."*

This physical therapist was, to me, the hands and feet of Jesus. Every week, he continued to speak truth over me, listened to me, and prayed for me. I began to see the heart of Jesus. God was not punishing me. He set me on a path of healing. I began to see the love the Lord had for me. Even though I was struggling, the Lord didn't leave me. He was walking with me through this because He loved me that much. I was being made perfect in love.

2 Corinthians 4:16–18

Therefore, we do not loose heart though outwardly we are wasting away, yet inwardly we are being renewed day by day. For our light and momentary trouble are achieving for us eternal glory that outweighs them all, so we fix our eyes not on what is seen, but on what is unseen, since what is seen is temporary, but what is unseen is eternal."

I went up for prayer a few times at the new church we have become a part of. I began to wonder, *Why wasn't God healing me right away?* As I asked, I heard the Lord, "Because I still have work to do."

God wants to heal my whole being, not just my physical body. He wants me to be whole—body, soul, and spirit. I was reminded of one of the pastor's wives I used to sit under. She was always so calm. She never rushed. She always listened quietly. When things were planned, it was never in a hurry. "Let's add it to the next calendar year," she would say. She had grace, and she moved about in peace. I loved that about her. She was the opposite of me.

I remember praying to the Lord a long time ago and asking Him to make me more like her. She walked in dignity and strength. *Proverbs 31:25–26* says, *"She is clothed with strength and dignity. She can laugh at the days to come.* This speaks of a wife to her husband, but it also applies to the church. I am learning. I have no choice. I can't talk a lot and I can't talk fast; I have to listen. I am learning to take things slow. I am learning balance. I have to. I have learned to live differently, to take things slower. As I do, my body has become a body at rest, like it always should have been. My prayer has been answered.

A LIFE WORTH SAVING

On some of those tough days, I would sometimes ask, "Why me?" I guess the better question would be why not me? *Second Corinthians 4:16–18 says, "Therefore we do not loose heart though outwardly we are wasting away, yet inwardly we are being renewed day by day. For our light and momentary trouble are achieving for us eternal glory that for outweighs them all, so we fix our eyes not on what is seen, but on what is unseen, since what is seen is temporary, but what is unseen is eternal."* The Lord was using this time to renew my strength, renew my soul, renew my spirit. *Romans 8:28 reads, "And we know that in all things God works for the good of those who love him, who have been called according to His purpose."* The Lord put so many people in my path, people I didn't even know, to walk this healing journey with me, to walk with me through this time in my life.

There are things I can't do right now. One thing I can't do is put a helmet on my head. This was a huge loss for me. It was something my husband and I did together. It's funny the first time I rode on the back of the bike—I found myself worshipping and praising God. It brought me inner peace and joy. Seeing God's creation from the back of a bike is an experience I will always treasure. It was a place I worshipped God for just being God, in all His glory.

I can't raise my hands in worship, and I can't sing out loud to the Lord as I used to, like I long to do. This was heartbreaking. I felt all the things that brought me close to God were being taken away from me. One day at church, I looked over at my husband, so full of sadness. I said, "I can't worship anymore."

He turned to me and said, "Yes, you can. It's just going to look a little different." In worship, I now stand, close my eyes, and lift my head to heaven. Somehow, I see myself. I see myself with my hands lifted high toward heaven. I can see the Spirit of the Lord all around. He is with me, and I am with Him. I am worshipping in spirit and in truth. It may not seem it and you may not see it, but the Lord does.

Through this, I've noticed that the Lord has given me back time, the one thing that always seems to get stolen. He has given it back to me. I had allowed Satan to take so much time from me as I rushed through life. I now take the time to brush my daughter's hair. I now take the time to scooch over and allow my daughter to jump in bed and cuddle. I now have time. Precious time that I will treasure.

As I have adjusted my life, it has enabled me to move forward. I needed to stop rushing through life. We all do. I learned that excitement and anxiety run on the same pathway. I had run on that for years. I have now learned how to calm that pathway. I no longer feel electricity running through my body all the time.

I am learning to live at a peaceful, even pace, one I never even knew existed. I choose every day what I'm going to do, and sometimes, I have to take breaks in between. I now have to use an automatic stapler and envelope opener at work. At home, I now have to use lightweight dishes that are lighter and easier to handle. I can no longer do all that I used to do in a day.

It's a blessing. I've slowed down enough that I have begun to notice people. I now have more compassion and understanding for people. I see them. As much as this has been an adjustment for me, it has been a blessing. I am going to continue to move forward in faith, knowing the Lord is with me, He is in me, and He has not left me. *Deuteronomy 31:6* says, *"Be strong and courageous, do not be afraid, for the Lord your God goes with you; He will never leave you nor forsake you."*

John 8:36

So, if the Son sets you free you will be free indeed.

My daughter had her graduation in Texas. I so badly wanted to go, but I was nervous. I prayed about my neck. I wanted to go, but I didn't want to risk any more injury. I was nervous to stay in a hotel, and I was nervous to go out to dinner.

Over the last few years, I had developed allergies. They would present themselves when I stayed in some hotels. It could be something they cleaned with or something they put through the air. At one hotel, I had to leave and sleep in the car because I couldn't breathe. I have had food allergies as well. I had to stop eating at restaurants. How was I to go to Texas to support my daughter?

As I prayed, the Lord brought to mind a song by Elevation worship, "Graves to Gardens." As I continued to pray, the Lord began to speak to me. He told me to bury my past. In my mind's eye, I could see the soil being moved away. He told me to bury all that I have gone through over the years. Bury it all. Burying it all seemed to me opposite of what the Lord would do. "Lord, why would you ask me to bury all this? Don't you want me to bring it all to the light?" Job 12:22 (ESV) says, *"He uncovers the deeps out of darkness and brings deep darkness to light."*

He replied, "You have. Now it's time to let it go." He said, "These things you are holding are graves. They bring death, not life. Bury them, and I will turn all your graves into gardens." As I listened to Him, I could see fresh dirt that had been placed over all the areas of my past. I could see a fresh garden begin to appear. As I looked, I could see sprouts forming, then flowers began to grow. The garden was in full bloom.

I thought about my youngest daughter. The Lord had showed me a picture of this beautiful flower that was within her. He showed me that every time it began to grow, something would come along and cut it down. I am praying and beginning to see that beautiful flower that is within her is starting to grow in her life as well. *Isaiah 51:3* reads, *"The Lord will surely comfort Zion and will look with compassion on all her ruins; he will make her deserts like Eden, her wasteland like the garden of the Lord. Joy and gladness will be found in her, thanksgiving and the sound of singing."*

The Lord is in the business of breathing new life in us. *Ezekiel 37:4–5* says, *"Then he said to me, 'Prophesy to these bones and say to them, "Dry bones, hear the word of the Lord! This is what the Sovereign Lord says to these bones; I will make breath enter you and you will come to life.""'*

I continued to pray and ask the Lord for an answer about the Texas trip. My physical therapist had told me he didn't sense any issues with me going and he believed I would be fine, but I was still a bit anxious. I needed more. A few days later, I received a call at work from a new customer. As we spoke, we realized we were both Christ followers. We started sharing about God, and after a while, my trip to Texas came up in our conversation.

I shared how I was a bit nervous about the plane. He asked me, "What would you say to someone else who was feeling as you are?"

I thought for a moment, and I said, "I would tell them to have faith and to trust God."

He said, "Then go and believe that for yourself." He said something else that struck me. It was something my physical therapist had said to me. "Fear is not from God." Then he asked me that same question, "What's the opposite of fear?" I knew the answer this time. It's love. Love casts out all fear. The Lord was really wanting me to grasp how wide and how deep the love of Christ is. *Ephesians 3:16–19* says, *"I pray that out of his glorious riches he may strengthen you with power through his Spirit in your being, so that Christ may dwell in our hearts through faith. And I pray that you, being rooted and established in love, may have power, together with all the Lords' people, to grasp how wide and long and high and deep is the love of Christ, and to know this love that surpasses knowledge-that you may be filled to the measure of all the fullness of God."*

I moved forward in faith and went on that trip. It was wonderful! After I was home for a few days, I began thinking of my trip and what a great time we all had as a family celebrating. I was blessed. The Lord quietly spoke to my heart as I was pondering all we had done. Beautifully, I heard the Lord speak, "You traveled. You flew on a plane. You stayed at a hotel, and you went out to dinner in a restaurant. Did I not tell you I could do more than you could ever ask or imagine?" I was humbled. The realization that the very thing the Lord told me He would do for me, He did. The Lord is faithful! The Lord is trustworthy! Things I would have never been able to do, I was doing! *Second Corinthians 3:17 says, "Now the Lord is the Spirit, and where the Spirit of the Lord is, there is freedom."*

The Lord wasn't only concerned about my physical body; He was concerned about my entire being. He wanted me living in complete freedom. Only the freedom that comes from Christ can truly set you free. *John 8:36 says, "So if the Son sets you free you will be free indeed."*

Job 42:10

After Job had prayed for his friends, the Lord restored his fortunes and gave him twice as much as he had before.

I was receiving counsel from the people the Lord put in my life: my family, the medical professionals, the church we were attending, and even strangers. The Lord had put them all in my life. All these people were put in my life at the right time. The Lord had all my days laid out for me. He was working on me, healing me. He brought people around me that encouraged me and, in some cases, told me the truth in love. We all need people like this in our lives.

As I continued in my daily time with the Lord, He led me to the book of Job. As I read the book of Job, I read of the friends that came to Job's side. At the beginning, they were silent, and then they began to speak. Some gave good godly advice, encouraging and caring, and some advice given were not so good. There became a point Job's friends began to not speak the truth about the Lord. The Lord was angry at them, and He told Job to pray for his friends.

As Job prayed for his friends, the Lord accepted his prayers. What the Lord showed me was that while Job was still in turmoil, the Lord called Job to pray for his friends. While Job was still struggling, the Lord called him to pray for others. As I read further down in verse 10, it says, *"After Job prayed for his friends the Lord restored his fortunes and gave him twice as much as he had before."*

Over these last few years, I had been focused on praying for myself, for my healing. Now the Lord was calling me to pray for others. I sensed that as I turned my prayers toward others and kept the focus off myself, my healing would continue to come. Later in *Job 4:12*, it says, *"The Lord blessed the latter part of Job's life more that the former part."* I receive that truth!

The Lord brought me to Job to teach me what comes next. Step by step, as I continue to seek the Lord, He continues to guide. He continues to give me hope every step of the way.

Who else do we have but the Lord? *Philippians 1:6* says, *"Being confident of this, that he who began a good work in you will carry it on to completion until the day of Christ Jesus."* This is the hope we have in Jesus!

As I began to question God about who I was to pray for, the Lord brought me to a study on prayer. I continued to pray for my children and my family, but I knew he wanted me to pray more. We continued to step out in faith and joined the group. It was there that prayer for others in faith began to rise. As we prayed for others, others lifted us up. The Lord continued to guide my path forward as I focused on Him and submitted to His will.

He has made me more aware of the people around me. He has given me compassion for and understanding of other people's struggles and difficulties. As I was walking the other day, I noticed a man, a hardworking man. I could tell that he had just left work and stopped to pick up materials. He walked with a limp. The Lord softened my heart as I walked by him, and I began to pray for him. The Lord softened my heart again later in the day when I noticed a woman. She, too, was suffering from an ailment. I've become more aware, more sensitive to the people around me as I slow down and listen to the Holy Spirit within.

> *I urge you, first of all, to pray for all people. Ask God to help them; interceded on their behalf and give thanks for them. (1 Timothy 2:1 NLT)*

Romans 8:1–2

There is now no condemnation for those who are in Christ Jesus because through Christ Jesus the law of the Spirit who give life has set you free from the law of sin and death.

This story is a story of one who was lost and now is found. This is a story of one, who even though has been found, still stumbles. This is a story of one who gave her life to Christ but, in her humanness, still seems to fail. We will never be perfect, but we are being renewed day by day. *Second Corinthians 4:16 says, "Therefore we do not lose heart. Though outwardly we are wasting away, yet inwardly we are being renewed day by day."*

As I listened to the pastor of our church the other day, he asked a question, "Who is Jesus?" If we fully believe in who God is, we will live a different life, one of freedom. Jesus is our teacher. He is our healer, and He guides us. If we can truly grasp who Jesus is, we will live life to the fullest, becoming all we were created to be, nothing holding us back. We would move forward knowing that the Lord is with us, teaching us, healing us, and encouraging us to use the calling He has put on our lives.

However, if we only believe a part of who God is, then we will only live a life that is the partial potential of who God created us to be. If we are not sure of who God is and we don't believe all of who He says He is, then we will wither, become fruitless, and barren. Move forward in faith knowing who God is. He is placing dreams in your heart, and He will bring you through every step of it. Have faith! Do not minimize what He has put on your heart, whether He spoke to you today or years ago.

In my quiet scripture meditation and prayer time, a question arose. *How can I show God that I love Him?* I had never thought of that question. We think so much about God's love for us and all He can do for us; do we ever think or ask what God would want from us? How can we show God that we love Him? As I thought about this, an overwhelming sense of peace flooded over me. "Trust."

Psalm 28:7 says, *"The Lord is my strength and my shield; my heart trusts in him, and he helps me. My heart leaps for joy, and with my song I praise him"* The answer came immediate and quick. "Trust Him." That's powerful. Do we trust Him to bring to completion all that He has called us to do? We show love to the Father by fully trusting in Him and never doubting. Faith.

First Peter 1:8–9 says, *"Though you have not seen him, you love Him; and even though you do not see him now, you believe in him and are filled with an inexpressible and glorious joy, for you are receiving the end result of your faith, the salvation of your souls."* We will show our love for Him when we stop doubting, when we stop worrying, when we start trusting Him.

The Lord confirmed all this in me when the pastor shared the big idea at the end of the church service. He said, "What we believe and say about who Jesus is has a profound impact on how He is able to impact our life." *First Thessalonians 5:24* says, *"The one who calls you is faithful, and he will do it."*

We do not need to be perfect for God to use us; we only need to be faithful. Think about your life. Where have you seen His hand guiding you, helping you? Meditate on all the Lord has done for you and all He has brought you through. As we remember, our faith in Christ is renewed and strengthened.

> *I will remember the deeds of the Lord; yes, I will remember your miracles of long ago. I will consider all your works and meditate on all your mighty deeds. Your ways, God are holy. What god is as great as our God? You are the God who performs miracles; you display*

your power among the people. With your mighty arm you redeemed your people, the descendants of Jacob and Joseph. (Psalm 77:11–13)

1 Corinthians 16:23 MSG

Our master Jesus has his arms wide open for you.

Why am I a life worth saving? *John 3:17* says, *"For God did not send his Son into the world to condemn the world, but to save the world through Him."* Because God thinks my life is a life worth saving. He didn't come to condemn the world! He came to save us!

Look at my life. Did he condemn me? *No!* In these pages, I share the story of my life, the good and the not-so good. I have done things that would justify condemnation—we all have—but God! God is not here to condemn us. He came to save us. Why? Because He loves us that much. He loves you that much.

Why is my life a life worth saving? My life is a life worth saving because God created me to have relationship with Him. My sin separates me from God. That's why He sent Jesus. His blood shed on the cross now covers my sin. God now sees me through the blood of Jesus. He no longer sees my sin. *Hebrews 9:14 (ESV)* says, *"How much more will the blood of Christ, who through the eternal Spirit offered himself without blemish to God, purify our conscience from dead works to serve the living God."*

Why is your life a life worth saving? Because you too are a child of God. He created you and He longs to have a personal relationship with you. Why? Because He loves you. *Micah 7:19* says, *"You will again have compassion on us: you will tread our sins underfoot and hurl all our iniquities into the depths of the sea."* The Lord knows. He sees you. We are sons and daughters of the Most High God. He loves you! Talk to your Father. Share with Him all that's on your heart and in your mind. Call out to Him. He's there.

The greatest story in the Bible that represents God's love for us is in Luke. It's about the prodigal son. *Luke 15:11–13* says, *"Jesus continued; 'There was a man who had two sons. The younger one said to the father, "Father, give me my share of the estate." So he divided his property between them. Not long after that, the younger son got together all he had, set off for a distant country and there squandered his wealth in wild living.'"* He took his inheritance from his father, left, and went and lived out his own life separate from the father. We do that, don't we?

After he squandered it all, he came back to his father. In *Luke 15:18–20*, it reads, *"I will set out and go back to my father and say to him: Father, I have sinned against heaven and against you. I am no longer worthy to be called your son; make me like one of your hired servants. So he got up and went to his father."* When the son acknowledged his sin, he went to his father to repent.

In *verse 20–24*, we see the heart of our Father. *"But while he was still a long way off, his father saw him and was filled with compassion for him, he ran to his son, threw his arms around him, and kissed him. The son said to him, 'Father, I have sinned against heaven and against you. I am no longer worthy to be called your son.' But the father said to the servants, 'Quick! Bring the best robe and put it on him. Put a ring on his finger and sandals on his feet. Bring the fatted calf and kill it. Let's have a feast and celebrate. For this son of mine was dead and is alive again; he was lost and is found.'"*

His father responded as our Father in heaven responds to us when we come to him. That is who our Father is. If we turn toward Him, He will run toward us. This is your heavenly Father. Your life is a life worth saving, so much so that God sent His son to die so that you may have life and have it for eternity. We are all a life worth saving. Come to Him! He's waiting for you!

John 3:16

For God so loved the world that he gave his one and only Son, that whoever believes in him should not perish but have eternal life.

God created us in His image. *Genesis 2:7* says, *"And the Lord God formed man from the dust of the ground and breathed into his nostrils the breath of life; and man became a living soul."* God loves you and wants you to experience peace and eternal life. He gave us free will, our own will, he gave us the freedom to choose. He wants us to choose to love Him. *First John 4:19* says, *"We love him, because he first loved us."*

Sometimes, we choose our own way. This is what separates us from God. *Romans 3:23* says, *"For all have sinned and fall short of the glory of God."* Our choice to sin separates us from God. Adam and Eve had free will, a choice, and they brought sin into the world. *Romans 5:12* says, *"Therefore, just as sin entered the world through one man, and death through sin, and in this way death came to all people, because all sinned."* All of us sin. Not one of us doesn't.

> *There is a way that appears to be right, but in the end, it leads to death. (Prov. 14:12)*

> *Your iniquities have separated you from your God; your sins have hidden his face from you. (Isa. 59:2)*

Good news! There is a way to bridge that gap! God sent Jesus to die on the cross and, three days later, to rise again from the grave! When He did that, He paid the penalty for our sin and bridged the gap between us and God. God loves us that much! *First Timothy 2:5–6* says, *"For there is one God and one mediator between God and mankind, Christ Jesus who gave himself as a ransom for all people."* Jesus took on our sins and suffered and died on the cross. *First Peter 3:18* says, *"For Christ also suffered once for sins, the righteous for the unrighteous, to bring you to God."*

Put your trust in Jesus and receive Jesus Christ as your Lord and Savior. Accept His free gift of eternal life. *John 1:12* says, *"To all who receive him, to those who believed in his name, he gave the right to become children of God."*

If you would like to receive the gift of eternal life and the forgiveness of sin,

- Admit your need for a Savior.
- Acknowledge and be willing to turn from your sin.
- Believe that Jesus Christ died for you on the cross and rose from the grave.

> *If you declare with your mouth, Jesus is Lord, and believe in your heart that God raised him from the dead, you will be saved. (Romans 10:9)*

- Through prayer, invite Jesus Christ into your life through the Holy Spirit.

"Dear God, I know I'm a sinner and I need a Savior. I will never be perfect, and I have made mistakes. Lord, I humbly ask for your forgiveness. I believe Jesus is Your Son and I believe He died on the cross for the forgiveness of my sins. I believe you raised Him from the dead into life. I choose to trust Him as my Savior and follow Him for the rest of my days. Lord, I ask that you guide my life and help me to do your will. You created me for a purpose and that purpose is to Love you. I pray all this in Jesus's name. Amen"

Acknowledgments

Do you not know that in a race, all the runners run, but only one gets the prize? Run in such a way as to get the prize. Everyone who competes in the games goes into strict training. They do it to get a crown that will not last, but we do it to get a crown that will last forever. Therefore, I do not run like someone running aimlessly; I do not fight like a boxer beating the air. No. I strike a blow to my body and make it my slave so that after I have preached to others, I myself will not be disqualified for the prize.
1 Corinthians 9:24–27

I want to thank God for this story he has given me. I praise Him and thank Him for quietly nudging me along, never letting this book leave my heart, soul, and mind. He has given me the strength and encouragement to finish. *Second Timothy 4:7* says, *"I have fought the good fight, I have finished the race, I have kept the faith."*

It has taken me fifteen years to complete this book. I want to thank all the pastors and leaders and churches the Lord brought us to. There are no perfect churches, there are no perfect people, there is only one perfect God that brings all things together for His glory. If we let Him, He brings us on a journey of healing and restoration.

As I look back on all the people God has brought into my life, I can stand firm in knowing that I can call on any one of them at any time from any church, knowing that they will all be there. We are all in the same family of God. We are all connected through Christ. *Philippians 2:1–2* says, *"Therefore if you have any encouragement from being united with Christ, if any comfort from his love, if any common sharing in the*

Spirit, if any tenderness and compassion, then make my joy complete by being like-minded, having the same love, being one in spirit and of one mind." We are all walking on our own journey, and we are all at different stages. Yet the journey has the same end—new life in Christ.

The Lord's timing is always perfect. I want to thank my family for the support they have given me during this time. Thank you, Michaela, for being the first to read and take on the challenge of editing this book for me! Thank you, Rebekah, for having a sensitive spirit and always checking in on me to see how I'm doing. Thank you, Olivia, for climbing on the bed numerous times and asking questions: Whatcha doing? Still writing that book? How long does it take you to write a book anyway? Always keeping me on my toes! To Matt, thank you for always reminding me I have a book to write when I would lose focus and wonder what it was God wanted me to do next.

Thank you, Lord, for restoring relationships throughout my life. You are faithful. *Jeremiah 30:17* says, *"But I will restore you to health and heal your wounds declares the Lord."*

> *Praise the Lord, my soul; all my inmost being, praise His holy name. Praise the lord, my soul, and forget not all His benefits-who forgives all your sins and heals all your diseases, who redeems your life from the pit and crowns you with love and compassion. (Psalm 103:1–4)*

About the Author

Corrine James has been a follower of Christ for thirty years. She has spoken at women's conferences, prayer breakfasts, and organized women's events. Over the years, she has hosted and led Bible studies and prayer groups. She has also been a youth leader.

The writer has sat under pastors and mentors and attended multiple women's conferences where she has continued to learn and grow as a Christ follower. She has shared her testimony multiple times via video and in person.

Recently, she took a step back from serving in the local church to fulfill the call the Lord put on her heart to write this book. Her hobbies are party planning, cake decorating, and spending time with her family. She is the mother of three beautiful daughters, and she has been married to her husband for twenty-eight years.

C.jamesps91@yahoo.com